Table of Contents
Science Enrichment
Grade 5

Flowers 2	Cough! Cough! 39
Food from the Sun 3	Body Trivia 40
Monocot or Dicot? 4	Solid to the Core? 41
Cone-Bearing Plants 5	Land Beneath the Ocean 42
Fiddleheads to Ferns 6	"Ping-Ping" 43
Nature's Green Carpet 7	Fire Rocks 44
Fungus Among Us 8	Stones of Sand 45
Baker's Buddy 9	Changing Rocks 46
Algae 10	Testing Minerals 47
A World of Plants 11	It's California's Fault! 48
Puzzling Plants 12	Ring of Fire 49
Classy Creatures 13	Shake, Rattle, and Roll! 50
Backbone or No Backbone 14	Mountain Building 51
Warm- and Cold-Blooded Animals 15	Natural Fountains 52
	Rivers of Ice 53
Invertebrates 16	Just Plain Dirt 54
Animals with a Double Life 17	Earth Shattering Review 55
Food Chains 18	Our Moon 56
Meat, Salad, and Casseroles 19	Changing Faces 57
Food Webs 20	Space Shadows 58
Gone for the Winter 21	Exploring Our Solar System 59
Endangered 22	Earth's Nearest Neighbors 60
The Tortoise and the Hare 23	The Outer Planets 61
Animal Facts 24	The Edge of the Solar System 62
Dem Bones, Dem Dry Bones" 25	Comets, Asteroids, and Meteors 63
Muscle Power 26	
Message Transmissions 27	The Solar System 64
Think Fast 28	Magnitude 65
Interbody Highway System 29	Star Heat 66
Team Work 30	A Star Is Born 67
Pick Up the Beat 31	Star Death 68
Respiratory System 32	Black Holes 69
Digestive System 33	Pictures in the Stars 70
Keep It Covered 34	The Zodiac 71
The Body's Camera 35	Space Puzzle 72
Catching Good Vibes 36	
Joe's Tooth: The Inside Story 37	
Nibblers and Chompers 38	**Answer Key (in middle of book)**

©1994 Instructional Fair, Inc.   1   IF0233 Science Enrichment

Flowers

Flowers have the important function of producing seeds. The male part of a flower is called the **stamen**. At the tip of the stamen is the **anther**, a tiny case with many grains of **pollen**. The female part of the flower is called the **pistil**. The tip of the pistil is the **stigma**, the long neck is the **style**, and the large base is the **ovary**. The ovary holds the tiny **ovules**, which develop into seeds.

Label the parts of the flower using the words in bold from above.

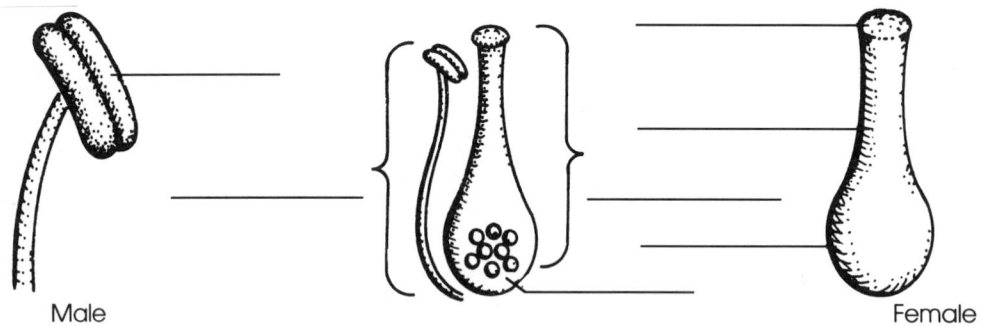

Male   Female

Complete each sentence with the missing word.

1. The anther is filled with __ __ __ __ __ __ .

2. The stigma is held up by the __ __ __ __ __ .

3. The female flower part is the __ __ __ __ __ __ .

4. Seeds form in the __ __ __ __ __ .

5. Seeds develop from tiny __ __ __ __ __ __ .

6. The tip of the pistil is the __ __ __ __ __ __ .

7. The male flower part is the __ __ __ __ __ __ .

Food from the Sun

With the help of chlorophyll and energy from the sun, a leaf can change lifeless substances into food. This process is called **photosynthesis**.

Plants need **water (H_2O)** and **carbon dioxide (CO_2)** to make food by photosynthesis. The water is gathered by the plant's roots. Carbon dioxide, found in the air, is gathered through tiny openings, called stomata, located on the underside of the leaf.

The leaf uses **chlorophyll** and **sunlight** to change water and carbon dioxide into oxygen and sugar. The sugar is mixed with water and sent to other parts of the plant. Oxygen is released into the air through the stomata.

Complete the formula for photosynthesis using the bold words above.
Photosynthesis =

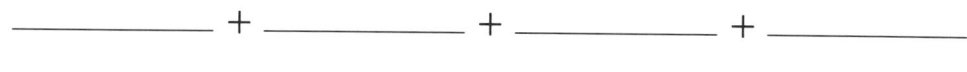

_____ + _____ + _____ + _____

Scott's dad gave him some healthy houseplants. Scott decided to keep them in his room, but his room was always dark. What do you think will happen to Scott's plants? Why?

_____

_____

_____

Sarah set up her aquarium with some fish and aquatic plants. Explain how the fish and the plants benefit from each other.

_____

_____

_____

Monocot or Dicot?

Flowering plants are divided into two main groups - the **dicots**, or dicotyledons, and the **monocots**, or monocotyledons. The basic differences can be found by looking at their seeds. The dicots have two cotyledons, or food parts, and the monocots have one cotyledon, or food part.

There are other differences in their leaves, stems, and flowers. The differences are noted in the chart below.

Plant Part	Monocot	Dicot
leaves	The veins are parallel.	The veins form a net-like structure.
stem	The bundles of tubes are scattered throughout the stem.	The bundles of tubes form a ring around the outside of the stem.
flower	The petals and stamen are in groups of three, six, and nine.	The petal and stamen are in groups of four and five.
seeds	The seeds have one cotyledon or food part.	The seeds have two cotyledons or food parts.

Identify each of the plant parts below as a dicot or monocot.

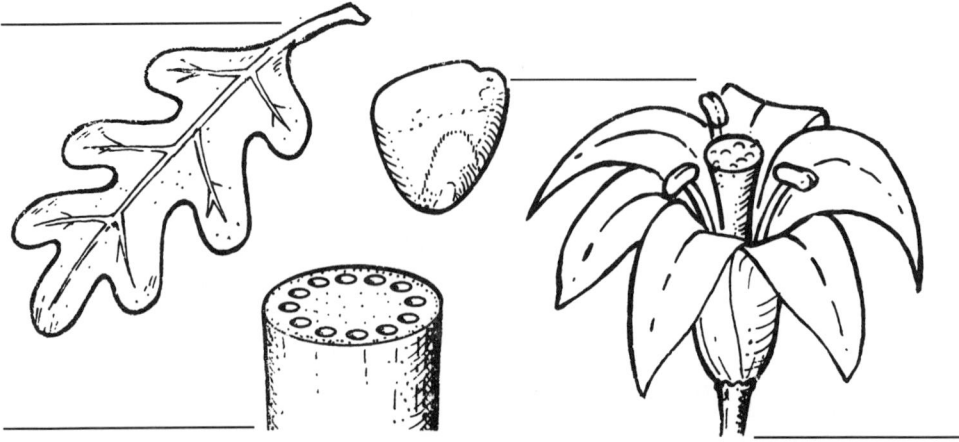

Something Special
Find some common plants around your home or school and classify them as monocot or dicot.

Cone-Bearing Plants

Plants, like pine trees, that develop seeds in cones are called **conifers**. Conifers have two kinds of cones. The smaller male cone develops pollen grains. Egg cells develop in the ovule of the much larger female cone. Pollen from the male cone is carried by the wind and lodges in the scales of the female cone. A pollen tube grows down to the ovule, and a new seed is formed. After the seeds are ripe, the cone and the seed drop to the ground.

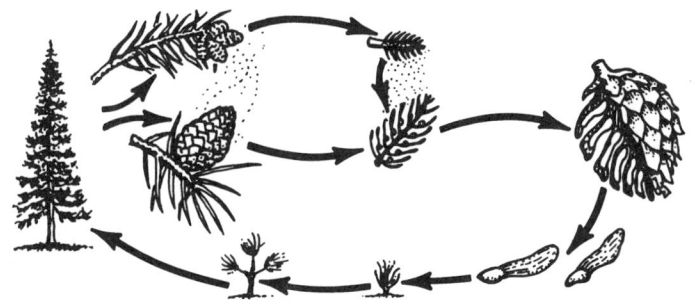

1. In what way is seed formation in a conifer the same as in a flowering plant? _____

   _____

2. How is seed formation in a conifer different than in a flowering plant? _____

   _____

Number the following steps in the correct order.

_____ A seed is formed.

_____ A new conifer sprouts from the seed.

_____ Pollen grains are carried by the wind.

_____ A pollen tube grows down to the ovule.

_____ Pollen grains lodge in the scales of the female cone.

_____ Ripened seeds are released from the cone.

Fiddleheads to Ferns

Have you ever seen little green ``fiddleheads'' growing out of the moist soil? These will soon be beautiful **ferns**. Ferns, like flowering green plants, have roots, stems, and leaves. Ferns reproduce from **spores**. Most ferns are about 25 cm tall, but some are as tall as trees!

Tiny brown dots, containing hundreds of spores, line the underside of the fern leaf. Spores that fall on a wet place grow into tiny heart-shaped plants. Each tiny plant produces both the sperm and the egg cells. After a rain, the sperm cell will swim to the egg cell through the water. When the sperm fertilizes an egg cell, a new young fern will grow. Making food by photosynthesis, the young fiddlehead will grow into a mature plant.

Complete the chart using information from above.

Plant parts	
How the fern makes food	
Size of plant	
Method of reproducing	

1. Why must ferns live in wet places? _____

2. How are ferns different than flowering plants? _____

© 1994 Instructional Fair   IF0233 Science Enrichment

Nature's Green Carpet

Have you ever seen a smooth, green, velvety carpet growing on a moist forest floor? This carpet is made of hundreds of tiny **moss** plants growing closely together.

Mosses, like ferns, do not produce seeds; they reproduce with spores. Sperm cells and egg cells are formed at the top of the moss plant. After a rain, the sperm travels through the water to the egg cell. The fertilized egg cell sprouts a tall stalk with a case for the spores at its tip. These spores will produce new mosses. Mosses make their food by photosynthesis, but unlike other green plants, they do not have roots, leaves or stems. Food and water travel slowly from cell to cell.

Complete the chart using the information from above.

Plant parts	
How it gets its food	
Size	
Method of reproducing	

1. Why must mosses live in wet places? _____

2. How are mosses like ferns? _____

3. How are mosses different from other green plants? _____

Fungus Among Us

A **fungus** plant is not a true plant, because it does not have roots, **stems**, **leaves**, or **chlorophyll**. **Fungi** cannot make their own **food** like green plants. Instead, they get their energy by absorbing food from dead or living matter.

Most fungi reproduce by forming **spores**. The spores fall on dead organisms. A tiny cell breaks out of the spore and grows into fuzzy threads. The threads form new caps, stalks, or capsules.

Fungi are helpful members of nature's recycling team. They help break down dead organisms that can then become part of the **soil**.

Complete the following sentences using the words in bold.

1. Most fungi reproduce by forming __ __ __ __ __ __ .
                                                         7

2. Fungi do not have roots, __ __ __ __ __ ,
                                            1   3

   or __ __ __ __ __ __ .

3. Fungi cannot make their own __ __ __ __ .
                                                 6

4. Fungi are not green; they lack

   __ __ __ __ __ __ __ __ __ __ __ .
           5   4

5. Mold and mushrooms are types of __ __ __ __ __ .
                                             2

6. Fungi break down dead organisms that then become part

   of the __ __ __ __ .

Use the numbered letters to solve the riddle.
"What kind of room has no walls, windows, or doors?"

__ __ __ __ __ __ __ __
1 2 3 4 5 6 7 1

Baker's Buddy

Yeast is another kind of fungus. Yeast differs from other fungi in two ways. First, yeast is made of only one cell. Second, yeast can reproduce in two ways. Each cell can grow a small bump, called a **bud**. When this bud grows large enough, it breaks off and forms a new cell. This is called **budding**. The second way of reproducing is when the cell divides two or three times inside the cell case. The new cells become spores and stay inside until the case breaks open.

Yeast grows rapidly when it has sugar for food. When yeast breaks down the sugar, it gives off carbon dioxide gas bubbles and alcohol. These bubbles cause bread dough to swell up. Yeast really is a baker's buddy!

Answer the following questions by unscrambling the letters in each yeast cell. The letters will ''bud'' into the correct answers.

1. Yeast is a kind of _____.

2. Yeast is made of only one _____.

3. Reproducing by making little bumps is called _____.

4. Yeast divides in the cell case and forms _____.

Find Out
Find out what Matzo is. How does it get its name?

Algae

Algae is one of the simplest forms of plant life. Like fungus, algae does not have roots, stems, or leaves. Unlike fungus, algae has chlorophyll and can make its own food by photosynthesis.

Algae can range in size from single cells in your aquarium to the giant Pacific kelp that grows to a length of sixty centimeters!

Complete the chart using the above information.
Size
How it makes food
Habitat
Plant parts

1. In what ways is algae similar to fungi? _____

_____

2. In what way is algae different than fungi? _____

_____

Find Out

Lichens are some of the plant world's most unusual organisms. Actually, lichens are two organisms - algae and fungi - that live together. Do some research on lichens. Why are lichens so unusual? Could algae and fungi survive alone? Explain.

A World of Plants

Scientists have a special way of classifying, or grouping, the many kinds of plants. Study the diagram below.

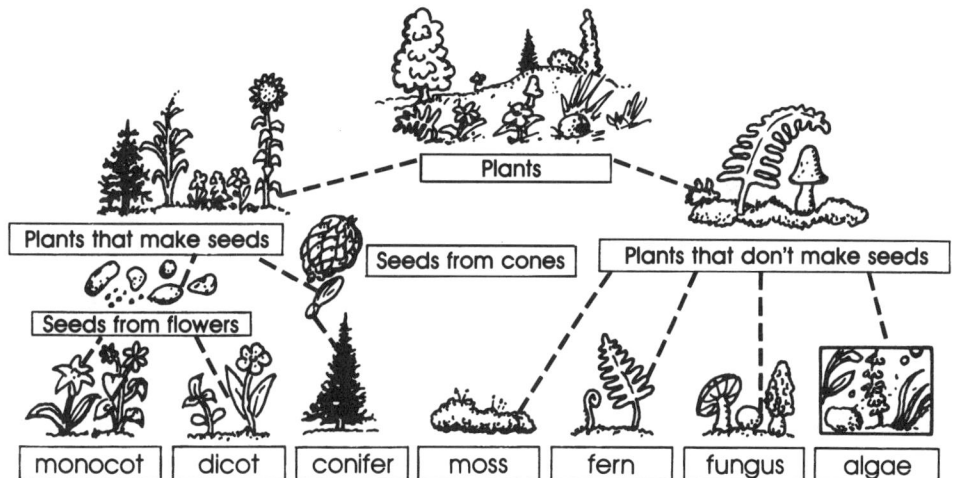

Look carefully at the plant characteristics listed below. Place a (✓) in the column or columns that represent the plant with that characteristic.

	monocot	dicot	conifer	moss	fern	fungus	algae
1. makes seeds							
2. makes seeds in a flower							
3. flower-made seed with two seed parts							
4. flower-made seed with one seed part							
5. makes seeds in a cone							
6. produces spores							
7. has leaves with veins							
8. has leaves with parallel veins							
9. has leaves with net-like veins							
10. has needle-like leaves							
11. one-celled plant							

Puzzling Plants

Complete the puzzle using words from the Word Bank.

Across
1. Gold dust found in the stamen
3. Makes seeds in a cone
4. Product of photosynthesis
7. Means of reproduction for ferns, molds, and yeast
8. See diagram.
11. Plant's food making process
12. See diagram

Down
1. See diagram.
2. See diagram.
3. Green coloring in leaves
5. See diagram.
6. See diagram.
7. See diagram.
9. See diagram.
10. Two food parts

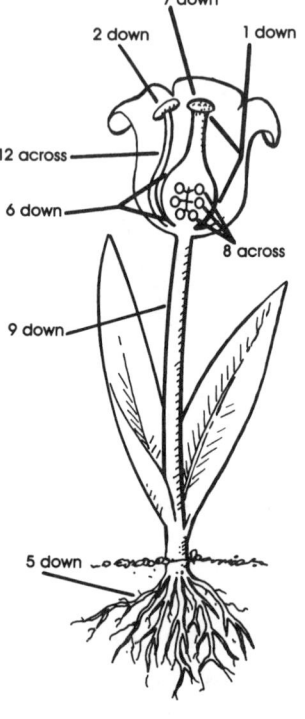

Word Bank
anther
chlorophyll
conifer
dicot
ovary
ovules
photosynthesis
pistil
pollen
root
spores
stamen
stem
stigma
sugar

Classy Creatures

___ ___ ___ ___ ___ ___ ___ ___

Scientists use a special tool to help them find the names of insects, trees, and many other things. It is called a **dichotomist key**.

Each of the creatures above has a name. We will use our own dichotomist key to give each creature its name. To use the key, work with only one creature at a time. First read steps 1a and 1b. Decide which statement is true about the creature. Then follow the directions after that step. The directions will lead you to a new pair of steps. Keep this up until you come to a step that gives you the creature's name. Write the creature's name in the space provided. After you have named all of the creatures, you will be able to complete the following sentence:

A dichotomist key is used to ___ ___ ___ ___ ___ ___ ___ ___ .

If this is true . . .	do this:
1 a. The creature has two eyes.	Go to step 2.
b. The creature has one eye.	Go to step 5.
2 a. The creature has one or more antennae.	Go to step 3.
b. The creature has no antennae.	Its name is "L."
3 a. The creature has one antenna.	Its name is "I."
b. The creature has more than one antenna.	Go to step 4.
4 a. The creature has two antennae.	Its name is "S."
b. The creature has three antennae.	Its name is "Y."
5 a. The creature has one or more antennae.	Go to step 6.
b. The creature has no antennae.	Its name is "A."
6 a. The creature has one antenna.	Its name is "F."
b. The creature has two antennae.	Its name is "C."

© 1994 Instructional Fair   IF0233 Science Enrichment

Backbone or No Backbone

The animal kingdom can be divided into two groups, **vertebrates** and **invertebrates**. Vertebrates are animals with backbones. The backbone is made of several bones called **vertebrae**. Each vertabra is separated by a thin disc of cartilage. The backbone supports the body and helps the animal move.

Some invertebrates, like crabs and lobsters, have hard, outer-body coverings. Some invertebrates, like worms, are soft all the way through their bodies.

Circle all of the hidden animals in the puzzle below. Then list them in their own group.

Word Bank

butterfly	skunk
cow	snail
crayfish	snake
deer	spider
dog	swan
fish	wasp
grasshopper	worm

```
N J W O R M E Z R A C D
G R A S S H O P P E R E
F K B P D S W A N P A E
S N A I L Q W C S X Y R
K E V D O G A I N C F G
U P S E A J S S A O I X
N O L R W M P H K F S C
K T F I S H G B E Y H O
U B U T T E R F L Y T W
```

Vertebrates   **Invertebrates**

Warm- and Cold-Blooded Animals

Mammals and birds are **warm-blooded** animals. Warm-blooded animals maintain a constant body temperature with the help of hair or feathers as insulation. Warm-blooded animals are called **endothermic** animals.

Cold-blooded animals, such as fish, reptiles, and amphibians, get their body heat from their surroundings. Their body temperature varies according to the temperature of their environment. Cold-blooded animals are called **ectothermic** animals.

Circle all the animals in the wordsearch below. Then list the animals in the proper group.

Word Bank

bear	rat
deer	salamander
duck	shark
eagle	snake
fox	toad
frog	trout
lizard	turtle
owl	

```
I  E  K  M  O  W  L  D  B  U
S  A  L  A  M  A  N  D  E  R
T  G  I  A  S  L  T  O  A  D
U  L  Z  F  II D  E  E  R  S
R  E  A  R  A  U  O  E  G  N
T  R  R  O  R  C  F  O  X  A
L  A  D  G  K  K  P  F  N  K
E  T  R  O  U  T  B  R  M  E
```

Warm-Blooded

Mammal	Bird

Cold-Blooded

Fish	Reptile	Amphibian

Invertebrates

Just three groups of the many kinds of invertebrates are listed below. The first group are **arthropods**. Arthropods are invertebrates with jointed legs. Insects, spiders, and crustaceans, like lobsters and crabs, belong to this group. **Worms** are slender, creeping animals with soft bodies and no legs. The last group are **mollusks**. Mollusks are also soft-bodied, but most have shells for protection. Some mollusks, like the octopus, do not have shells.

Find some examples of invertebrates in the puzzle below. Then list them under the group they belong to.

```
M F T A P E W O R M F
C R A Y F I S H O S L
L O B S T E R D U O A
A P L Q C M C H N C T
M T I U W O R A D T W
S N A I L T A J W O O
S K N D B H B E O P R
A N T O Y S T E R U M
E A R T H W O R M S O
```

Word Bank

ant	crayfish	lobster	oyster	squid
clam	earthworm	moth	roundworm	tapeworm
crab	flatworm	octopus	snail	

Arthropods   **Worms**   **Mollusks**

_____   _____   _____

_____   _____   _____

_____   _____   _____

_____   _____   _____

_____   _____   _____

Animals with a Double Life

Amphibians are cold-blooded vertebrates. The word **amphibia** means to live a double life. Some amphibians live exclusively on land or in the water, while others live in both habitats. Frogs, toads, and salamanders are three of the most common amphibians.

Adult frogs and toads are able to hear you sneak up on them because they have large eardrums, called **tympanums**. Salamanders do not have eardrums but sense vibrations through their legs.

Frogs and toads develop from eggs that are laid in the water. The larval forms of the frog and toad are called **tadpoles**. Salamanders hatch from eggs within the adult.

Use the pictures and information above to complete the chart. Make a (✓) in the correct box or boxes.

	Frog	Toad	Salamander
smooth skin			
bumpy skin			
nostrils			
tympanum			
tail			
strong hind legs			
backbone			
warm-blooded			
cold-blooded			

© 1994 Instructional Fair   IF0233 Science Enrichment

Food Chains

In the woodland and aquatic communities, there are a large number of food chains. Study the picture on this page.

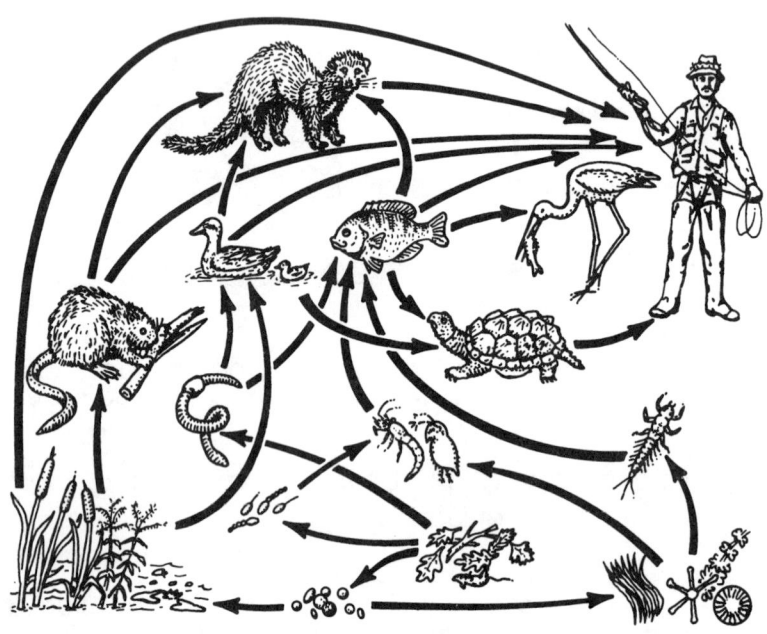

Find at least three food chains in the scene above. List the food chains below.

Food Chain #1   Food Chain #2   Food Chain #3

_____   _____   _____
_____   _____   _____
_____   _____   _____
_____   _____   _____
_____   _____   _____

Meat, Salad, and Casseroles

Animals and plants often get their food from different sources. Plants that make their food from sunlight, air, and water are called **producers**. Animals are **consumers**; they get their food from other sources. Animals that eat only plants are called **herbivores**. **Carnivores** are animals that eat only meat. **Omnivores** are animals that eat both plants and meat. Which of these are you?

Study the picture below. Then list all the carnivores, herbivores, omnivores, and producers that you can find.

Carnivore	Herbivore	Omnivore	Producer
_____	_____	_____	_____
_____	_____	_____	_____
_____	_____	_____	_____
_____	_____	_____	_____

Food Webs

Most animals, like humans, eat more than one kind of food. This means that most animals are members of more than one food chain. Separate food chains that interlock are called **food webs**.

Form a food web by drawing arrows from each prey to its predator. Remember - most prey have more than one predator. (Hint: Use a different colored crayon for each food chain.)

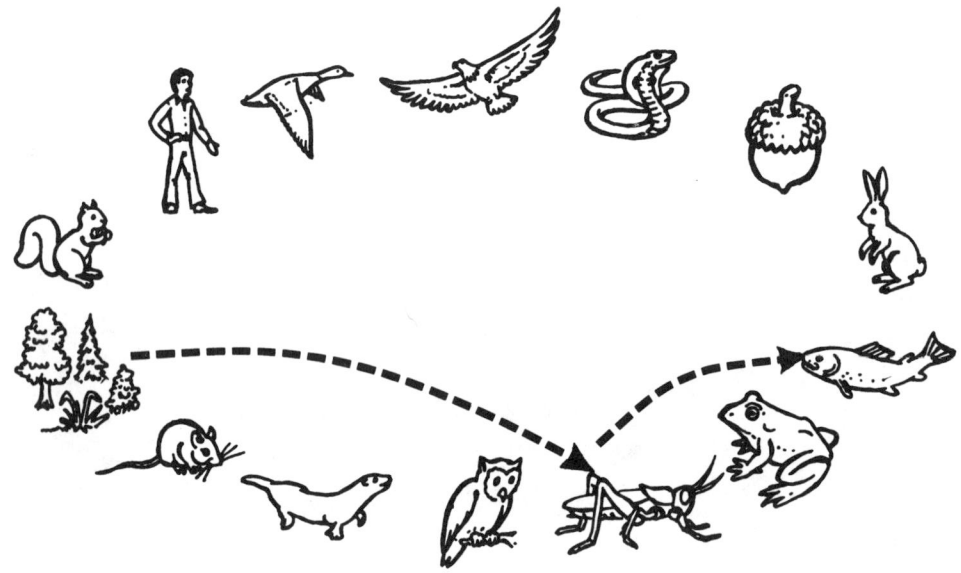

One food chain that you may have found in the food web is this one:

plant ➡ grasshopper ➡ trout ➡ otter

Write one more food chain that you found in your food web.

_____

_____

Gone for the Winter

When the cold winds blow, some animals travel to other regions for the winter. In the spring, they travel back to their summer habitat. This movement is called **migration**. Some animals migrate to warmer climates to find food. Others, like salmon and whales, migrate to give birth to their young.

Below are three pictures of migration. Choose one of the pictures and write a brief news article for the outdoor section of your newspaper. Use the five W's (who, what, where, when, and why) in your article.

Endangered

Today, thousands of animals are in danger of becoming **extinct**.

The jaguar, polar bear, sperm whale, and African elephant are only a few of the many animals that people have **endangered**. These animals are hunted for meat, fur, and trophies.

Some animals are endangered because their habitats are being destroyed by land development.

Most recently, man has polluted the environment with pesticides and fertilizers that have poisoned the food of many animals. Insecticides have entered the bald eagle's food chain, causing the now thin-shelled eggs to break before hatching.

Use another source to find out the names of some other animals that are endangered or extinct. Then fill in the chart below.

Animal	Endangered or Extinct	Why?

The Tortoise and the Hare

Many animals depend on their speed to escape from predators. Other animals use their speed to capture prey. Graph the speeds of these animals on the chart below from slowest to fastest. Then answer the questions below.

Animal	Speed (km per hour)
butterfly	19
elephant	40
coyote	72
cheetah	113
grizzly bear	48
housefly	8
salmon	48
sailfish	96
jack rabbit	64
lion	80
human (jogging)	11

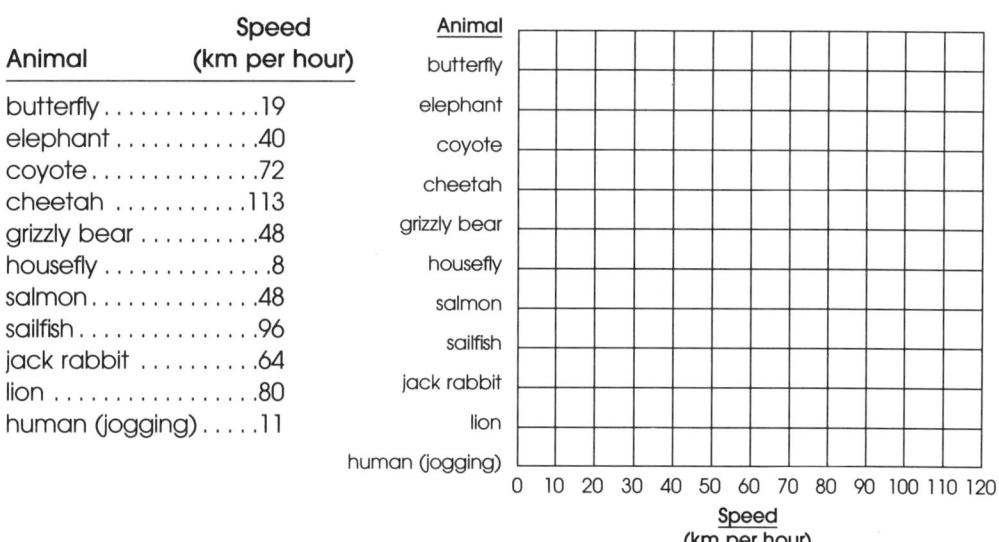

Both the coyote and the rabbit are very fast animals, but each uses its speed in a different way. How does each animal use its speed?

_____

_____

The tortoise is not very fast, but it has other adaptations to aid in protection. How does the tortoise protect itself?

_____

_____

Animal Facts

Finish the puzzle below.

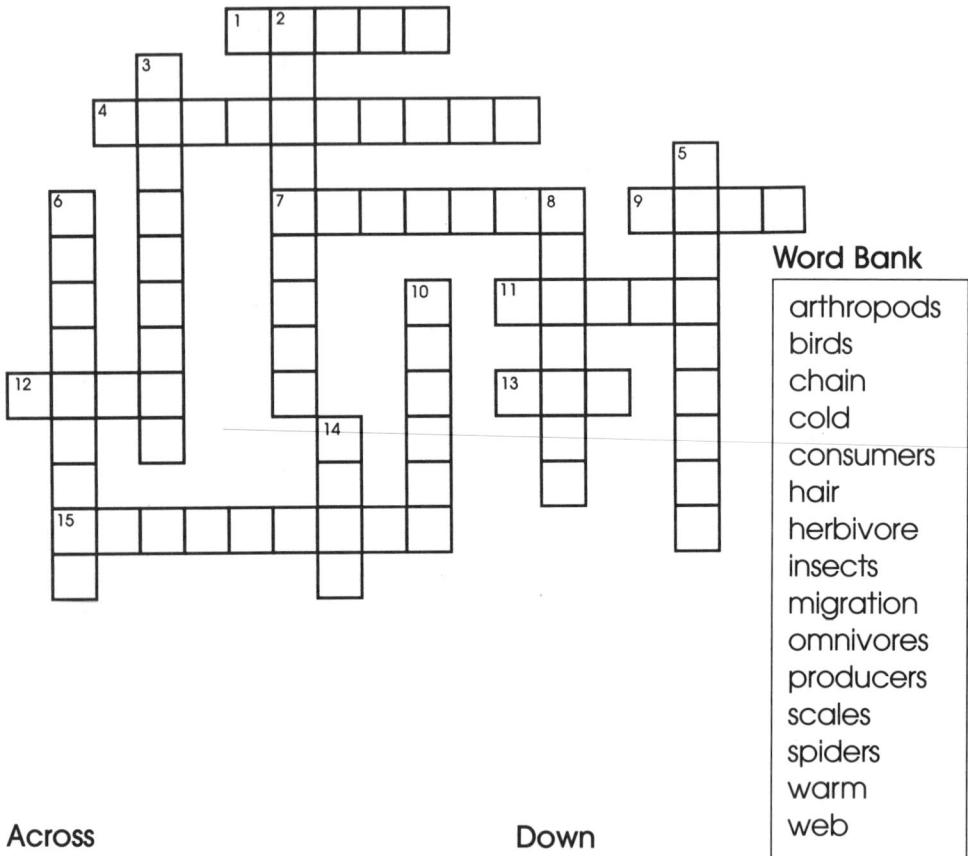

Word Bank

arthropods
birds
chain
cold
consumers
hair
herbivore
insects
migration
omnivores
producers
scales
spiders
warm
web

Across

1. A series of animals that feed on each other is a food _____ .
4. Invertebrates with jointed legs
7. Largest group of invertebrates
9. Reptiles are _____ -blooded.
11. Feathered, warm-blooded vertebrates
12. Body covering of mammals
13. Interlocking food chains form a food _____ .
15. Organisms that eat both plants and animals

Down

2. Animal that eats only plants
3. Organisms that make their own food
5. Organisms that do not make their own food
6. Seasonal movement of animals
8. Arthropods with eight legs, two body sections, and no antennae
10. Body covering of reptiles
14. Birds and mammals are _____ -blooded animals.

"Dem Bones, Dem Dry Bones"

Use your science book or another source to help.
Label the skeletal system with the scientific name for each bone.

Scientific Names

a. pelvis
b. vertebrae
c. scapula
d. cranium
e. radius
f. femur
g. mandible
h. tibia
i. patella
j. clavicle
k. coccyx
l. rib

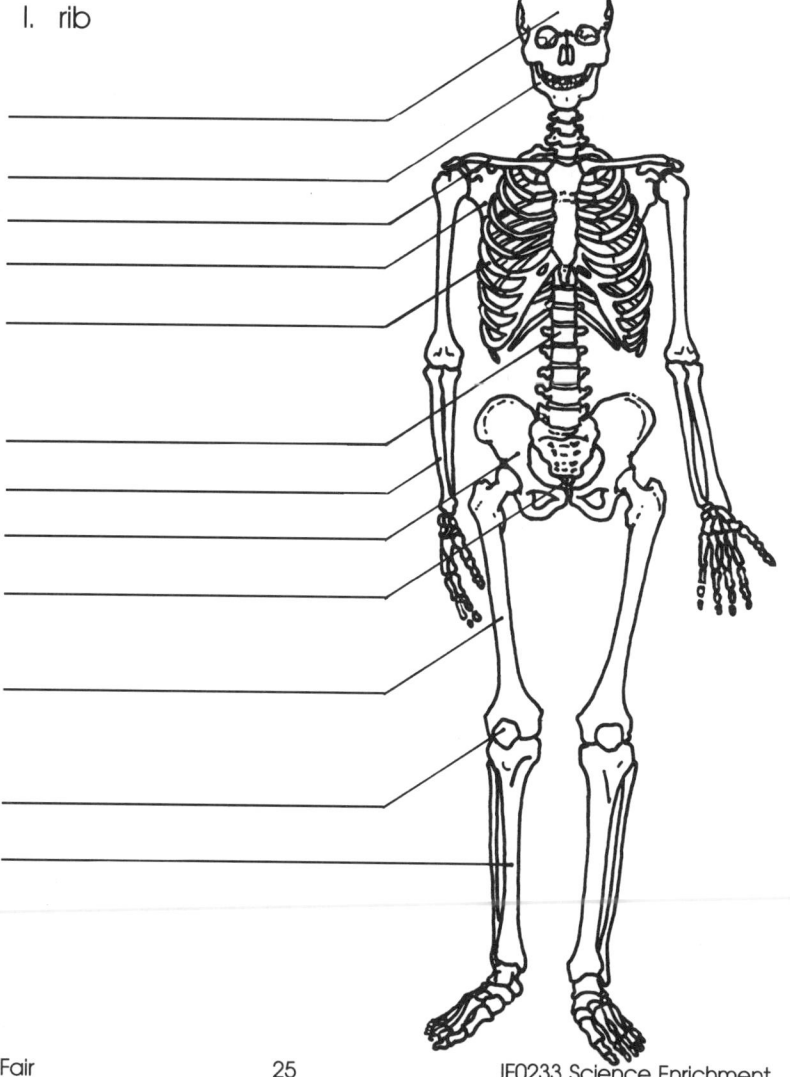

© 1994 Instructional Fair   IF0233 Science Enrichment

Muscle Power

Use your science book or another source to help.
Fill in the blanks with words from the Word Bank.

Word Bank
- involuntary
- voluntary
- smooth
- cardiac
- skeletal
- three
- tendons

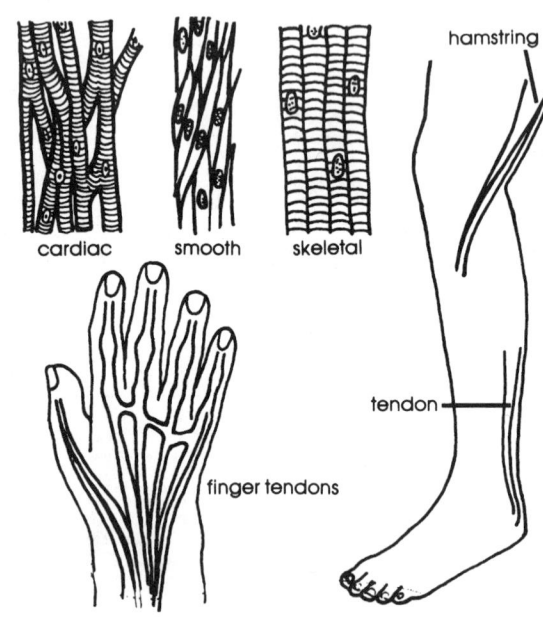

There are _____ kinds of muscles. Internal organs, such as the intestines, the stomach, and the esophagus are moved by the _____ muscles. The _____ muscles move your skeleton and external body parts. The heart beat is controlled by the _____ muscle. Muscles which need a special message from your brain in order to work are called _____ muscles. Muscles which move automatically, without conscious thought, are called _____ muscles. The tough cords that connect the skeletal muscles to your bones are called _____ .

Message Transmissions

Use your science book or another source to help. Fill in the spaces with words from the Word Bank.

Your body has its own system for sending messages to your brain. This system of individual nerves and their pathways is found throughout the body. It is called the **peripheral nervous system**. The peripheral nervous system is a pathway to the brain for your five senses. It also serves your internal organs and helps you respond to your environment.

Word Bank

| axons |
| dendrites |
| synapse |
| neurons |

Messages are sent to the brain through a network of nerve cells called _____.
Neurons have longs arms, called _____, and shorter arms, called _____.

In order for messages to travel along the pathway, the neurons must connect with each other. This connection is called a _____.
Messages enter each neuron through the dendrite. Messages exit the neuron through the axon.

Color the parts of the nervous system.

brain - gray
spinal cord - blue
nerves - red

© 1994 Instructional Fair

Think Fast

While riding your bike down the street, a car suddenly pulls out in front of you. Your eyes send a message to your brain. Your brain sends a message to your muscles to apply the brakes. How long did it take you to stop? This time is called your **reaction time**.

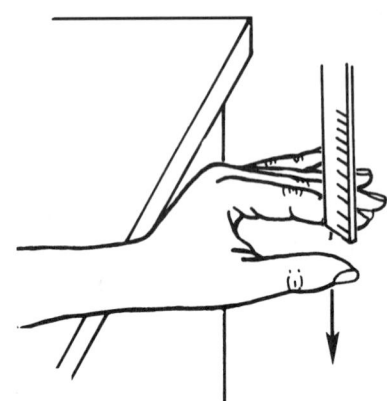

Here is a simple experiment to find out your **reaction time**. The only materials you will need are a 30 cm ruler and a partner.

1. Place your left arm on your desk with your hand over the edge.
2. Space your thumb and index finger apart a little more than the thickness of the ruler.
3. Your partner will hold one end of the ruler with the other end level with the top of your index finger.
4. Your partner will say ``ready,'' pause a few seconds, and drop the ruler.
5. Catch the ruler and check the distance by reading the level at the bottom of the index finger.
6. Record your results.
7. Now, try the experiment again with your right hand.

Trial	Left hand	Right hand
1		
2		
3		
4		
5		

Average: _____ _____

Which hand had the fastest reaction time?

_____

Fun Fact
Nerve impulses, or messages, travel at 100 meters per second!

Interbody Highway System

Veins, arteries, and capillaries are the blood vessels that form the fantastic highway system in your body.

Write **vein**, **artery**, or **capillary** in front of the statement that best describes the type of blood vessel.

1. _____ carries blood away from the heart.

2. _____ carries blood back to the heart.

3. _____ is the tiniest blood vessel.

4. _____ carries oxygen-rich blood.

5. _____ connects the veins and arteries.

Your blood is the vehicle that travels this highway. It transports oxygen, carbon dioxide, food, and waste. Your blood also fights infection and clots to prevent excessive blood loss.

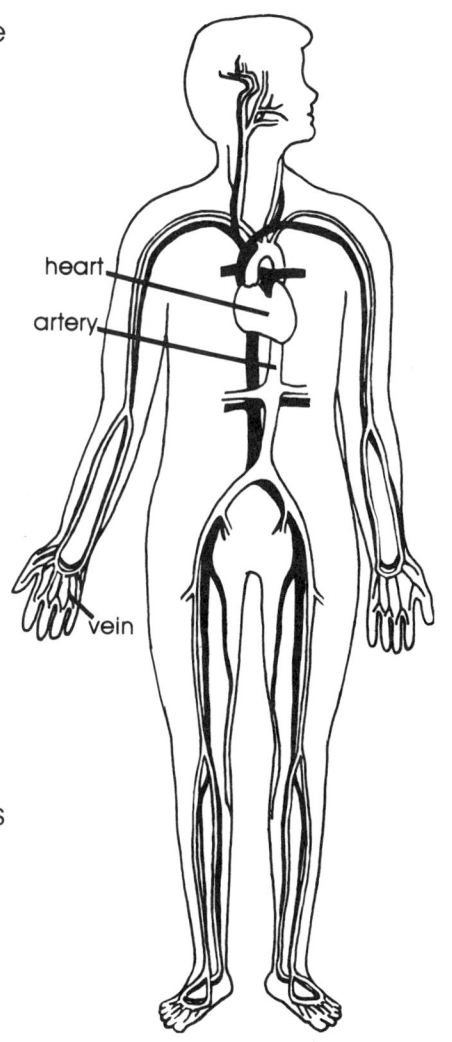

© 1994 Instructional Fair   29   IF0233 Science Enrichment

Team Work

Your heart is really two pumps that work together like a team. The right side of your heart takes dirty, carbon dioxide-filled blood in through the **right atrium** and **right ventricle**. It then pumps it through the **pulmonary artery** into your lungs. The blood is filled with oxygen in the lungs and passes through the **pulmonary vein** and into the **left atrium** and **left ventricle** on the left side of the heart. The left side of the heart then pumps this rich, oxygen-filled blood through the main artery of the body, called the **aorta**, to all the parts of your body.

Use arrows to trace the path of the blood.
Color the part of the heart filled with dirty, carbon dioxide-filled blood in blue.
Color the areas filled with oxygen-rich blood in red.

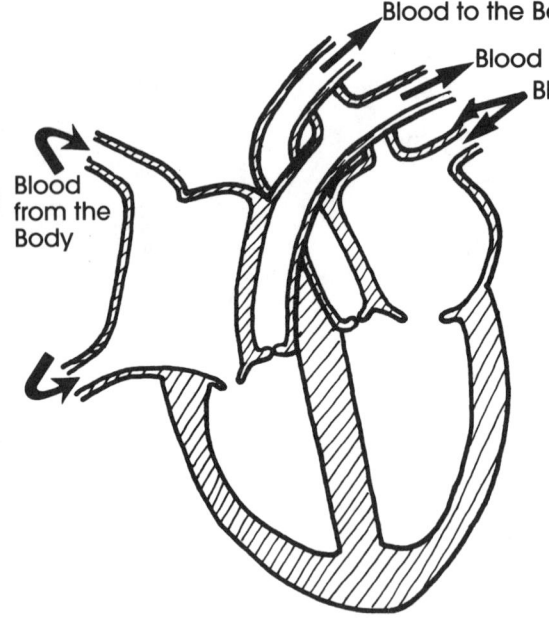

Activities that make you breathe deeply and your heart beat faster for 5 minutes or more are called **aerobic** activities. Aerobic means "using oxygen." These activities help strengthen your heart. Activities that are done quickly and don't require new supplies of oxygen are called **anaerobic** activities.

List aerobic and anaerobic activities that you enjoy.

Aerobic

1. _____
2. _____
3. _____
4. _____
5. _____

Anaerobic

1. _____
2. _____
3. _____
4. _____
5. _____

Pick Up the Beat

Your pulse is caused by the stopping and starting of the blood as it rushes through your arteries. You can feel your pulse at any spot an artery is near the surface of the skin. These spots are called **pulse points**. One pulse point is located on the inside of your wrist.

Name some other pulse points.

_____

_____

Your pulse rate changes during different kinds of activity. Check your pulse rate after doing these activities.

Activity	Pulse rate for 15 seconds	Multiply by 4	Pulse rate for 1 minute
sitting			
hopping 25 times			
hopping 100 times			
lying down			

How does your pulse rate change during exercise?

_____

Why do you think your pulse rate changes during exercise?

_____

Respiratory System

Your breathing, or respiratory, system is made of many parts. Solve the respiratory riddles using the Word Bank.

1. "I'm the windpipe that brings fresh air to your lungs."

   _____

2. "There are 600 million of us tiny air sacs in your lungs."

   _____

3. "Tra-la-la. I'm your voice box."

   _____

4. "We branch to the left and right from your windpipe."

   _____

5. "I enter your blood with each breath of fresh air."

   _____

6. "I help squeeze the air out of your lungs."

   _____

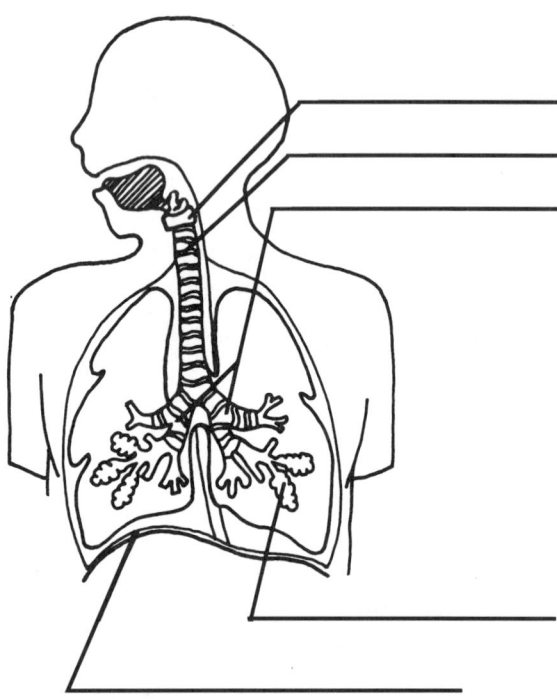

Label the diagram using the words from the Word Bank.

Word Bank

| alveoli |
| bronchial tubes |
| diaphragm |
| larynx |
| oxygen |
| trachea |

Digestive System

Use your science book and the Word Bank to help label the parts of the digestive system.

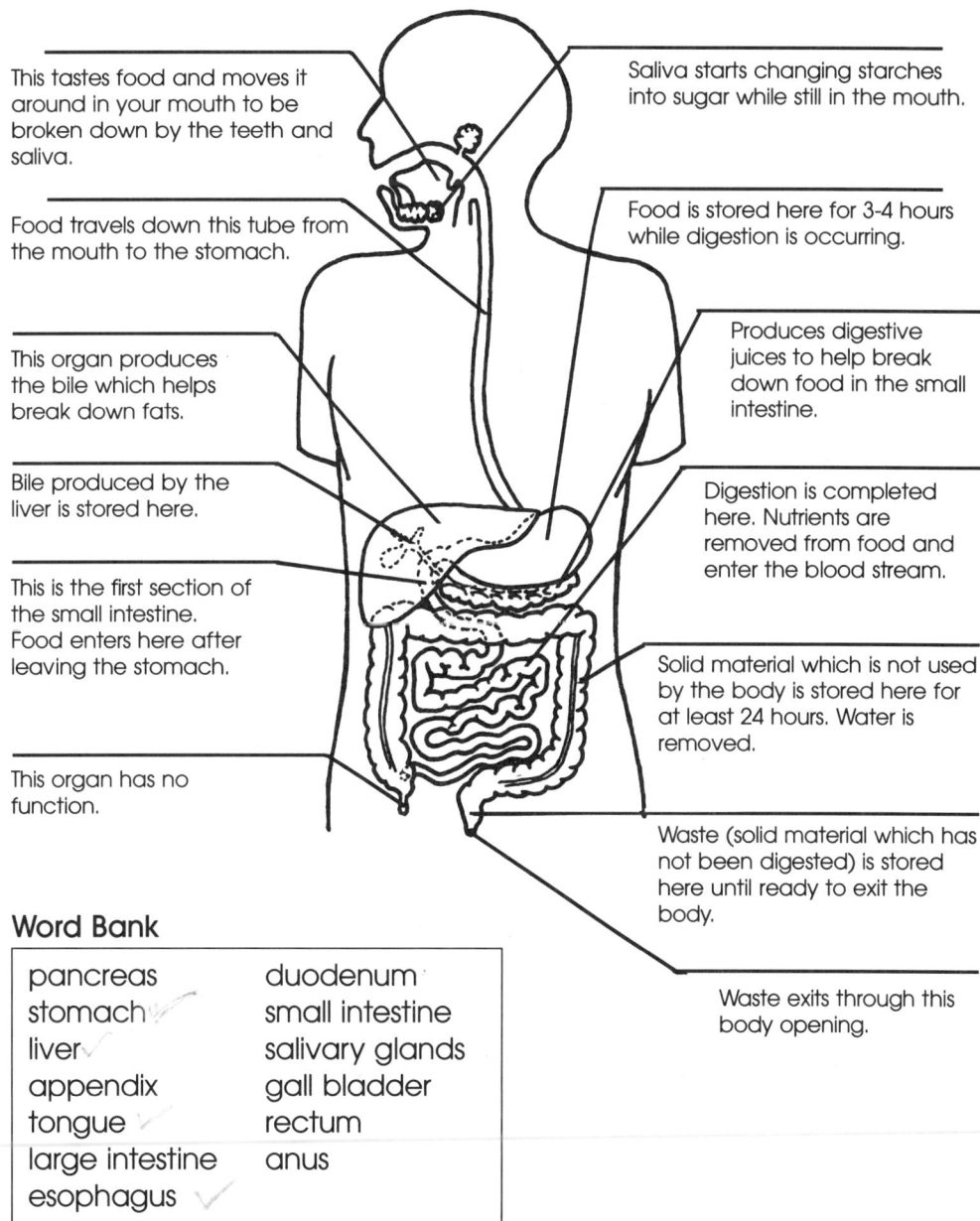

This tastes food and moves it around in your mouth to be broken down by the teeth and saliva.

Food travels down this tube from the mouth to the stomach.

This organ produces the bile which helps break down fats.

Bile produced by the liver is stored here.

This is the first section of the small intestine. Food enters here after leaving the stomach.

This organ has no function.

Saliva starts changing starches into sugar while still in the mouth.

Food is stored here for 3-4 hours while digestion is occurring.

Produces digestive juices to help break down food in the small intestine.

Digestion is completed here. Nutrients are removed from food and enter the blood stream.

Solid material which is not used by the body is stored here for at least 24 hours. Water is removed.

Waste (solid material which has not been digested) is stored here until ready to exit the body.

Waste exits through this body opening.

Word Bank

pancreas	duodenum
stomach	small intestine
liver	salivary glands
appendix	gall bladder
tongue	rectum
large intestine	anus
esophagus	

Keep It Covered

Your skin does more than cover your body. Your skin does three important jobs. It helps keep your body cool and comfortable. It is a sensor that warns you of danger. And it provides protection from dirt and bacteria.

Label the parts of the cross-section of the skin. Use another source to help.

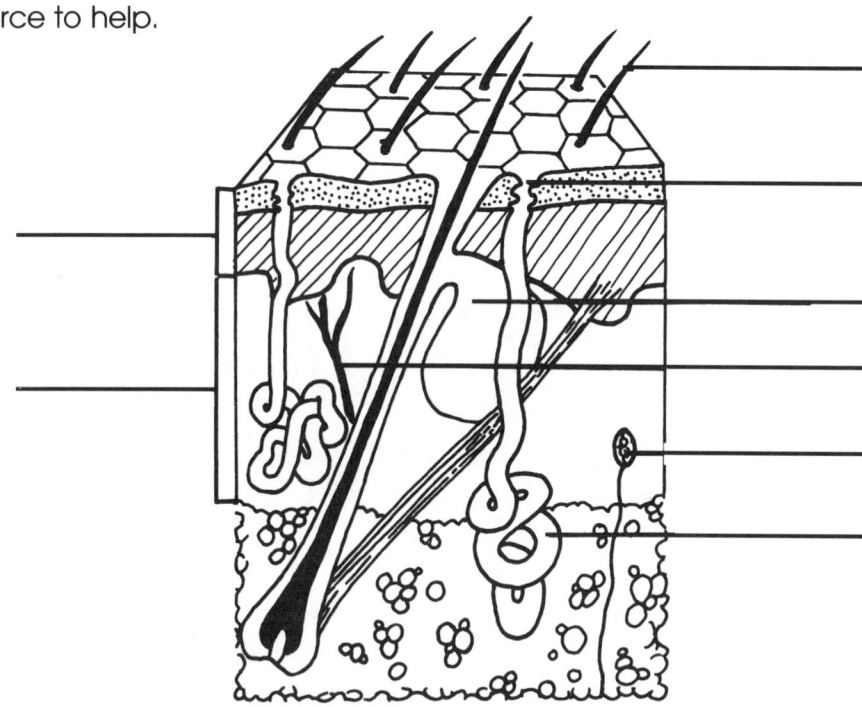

How does your skin help you in the following situations?

heat _____

dirt _____

pain _____

© 1994 Instructional Fair						IF0233 Science Enrichment

The Body's Camera

Use your science book or another source to help.
Label the parts of the eye with terms from the Word Bank.

Word Bank

| lens | optic nerve | pupil | sclera |
| cornea | iris | retina | vitreous humor |

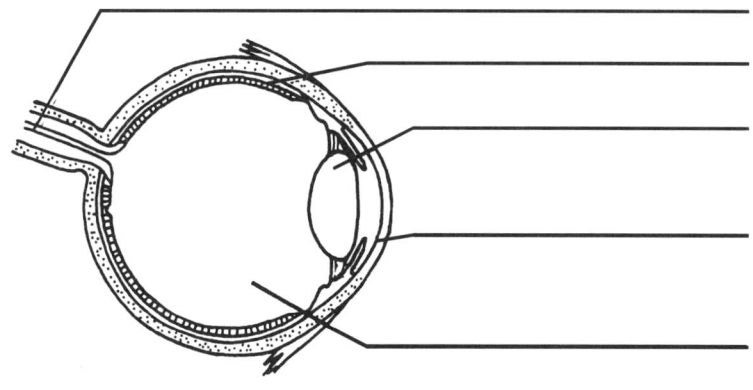

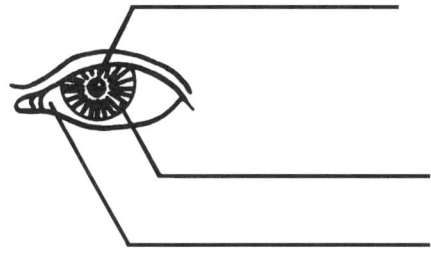

Something Special
Your retina is made up of light-sensitive cells that can be stimulated by pressure. Close your eyes and very gently press on them. The stars that you are seeing are called pressure flashes.

Catching Good Vibes

Use your science book or another source to help.
Complete the following sentences using the Word Bank.

The car honks its horn. The sound waves are collected by
your _____ and travel down the _____.
The sound strikes the _____ causing the tight skin to
vibrate. Three tiny bones called the _____,
_____, and _____ magnify
and send the sound to the inner ear. The sound travels to
the _____, a coiled, snail-shaped passage filled with
liquid and nerve hairs. The nerve hairs send signals through
the _____ to the brain.

Label the parts of the ear
using the Word Bank.

Word Bank

auricle
ear drum
auditory canal
auditory nerve
hammer
anvil
stirrup
cochlea

Answer Key

Science Enrichment

Grade 5

Flowers

Flowers have the important function of producing seeds. The male part of a flower is called the stamen. At the tip of the stamen is the anther, a tiny case with many grains of pollen. The female part of the flower is called the pistil. The tip of the pistil is the stigma, the long neck is the style, and the large base is the ovary. The ovary holds the tiny ovules, which develop into seeds.

Label the parts of the flower using the words in bold from above.

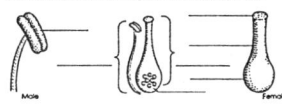

Complete each sentence with the missing word.
1. The anther is filled with **pollen**.
2. The stigma is held up by the **style**.
3. The female flower part is the **pistil**.
4. Seeds form in the **ovary**.
5. Seeds develop from tiny **ovules**.
6. The tip of the pistil is the **stigma**.
7. The male flower part is the **stamen**.

Food from the Sun

With the help of chlorophyll and energy from the sun, a leaf can change lifeless substances into food. This process is called photosynthesis.

Plants need water (H_2O) and carbon dioxide (CO_2) to make food by photosynthesis. The water is gathered by the plant's roots. Carbon dioxide, found in the air, is gathered through tiny openings, called stomata, located on the underside of the leaf.

The leaf uses chlorophyll and sunlight to change water and carbon dioxide into oxygen and sugar. The sugar is mixed with water and sent to other parts of the plant. Oxygen is released into the air through the stomata.

Complete the formula for photosynthesis using the bold words above.
Photosynthesis =
water + **carbon dioxide** + **chlorophyll** + **sunlight**

Scott's dad gave him some healthy houseplants. Scott decided to keep them in his room, but his room was always dark. What do you think will happen to Scott's plants? Why?
Scott's plants may become weak and may die. There is no sunlight for photosynthesis to occur.

Sarah set up her aquarium with some fish and aquatic plants. Explain how the fish and the plants benefit from each other.
Fish breathe in oxygen and out carbon dioxide. Plants take in carbon dioxide, and release oxygen.

Monocot or Dicot?

Flowering plants are divided into two main groups - the dicots, or dicotyledons, and the monocots, or monocotyledons. The basic differences are found in their seeds. The dicots have two cotyledons, or food parts, and the monocots have one cotyledon, or food part.
There are other differences in their leaves, stems, and flowers. The differences are noted in the chart below.

Plant Part	Monocot	Dicot
leaves	The veins are parallel.	The veins form a net-like structure.
stem	The bundles of tubes are scattered throughout the stem.	The bundles of tubes form a ring around the outside of the stem.
flower	The petals and stamen are in groups of three, six, and nine.	The petal and stamen are in groups of four and five.
seeds	The seeds have one cotyledon or food part.	The seeds have two cotyledons or food parts.

Identify each of the plant parts below as a dicot or monocot. 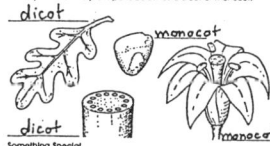
dicot **monocot** **dicot** **monocot**

Something Special
Find some common plants around your home or school and classify them as monocot or dicot.

Cone-Bearing Plants

Plants, like pine trees, that develop seeds in cones are called conifers. Conifers have two kinds of cones. The smaller male cone develops pollen grains. Egg cells develop in the ovule of the much larger female cone. Pollen from the male cone is carried by the wind and lodges in the scales of the female cone. A pollen tube grows down to the ovule, and a new seed is formed. After the seeds are ripe, the cone and the seed drop to the ground.

1. In what way is seed formation in a conifer the same as in a flowering plant? **The pollen grows to the ovule and a new seed is formed.**
2. How is seed formation in a conifer different than in a flowering plant? **Conifers have no flowers. They have male and female cones; most flowers have both the male and female parts in the same flower.**

Number the following steps in the correct order.
4 A seed is formed.
6 A new conifer sprouts from the seed.
1 Pollen grains are carried by the wind.
3 A pollen tube grows down to the ovule.
2 Pollen grains lodge in the scales of the female cone.
5 Ripened seeds are released from the cone.

Fiddleheads to Ferns

Have you ever seen little green "fiddleheads" growing out of the moist soil? These will soon be beautiful ferns. Ferns, like flowering green plants, have roots, stems, and leaves. Ferns reproduce from spores. Most ferns are about 25 cm tall, but some are as tall as trees!

Tiny brown dots, containing hundreds of spores, line the underside of the fern leaf. Spores that fall on a wet place grow into tiny heart-shaped plants. Each tiny plant produces both the sperm and the egg cells. After a rain, the sperm cell will swim to the egg cell through the water. When the sperm fertilizes an egg cell, a new young fern will grow. Making food by photosynthesis, the young fiddlehead will grow into a mature plant.

Complete the chart using information from above.

Plant parts	**roots, stems, leaves**
How the fern makes food	**photosynthesis**
Size of plant	**25 cm. ave. to tree height.**
Method of reproducing	**reproduce from spores**

1. Why must ferns live in wet places? **To reproduce, the sperm cell must be able to swim to the egg cell.**
2. How are ferns different than flowering plants? **They reproduce with spores, not seeds.**

Nature's Green Carpet

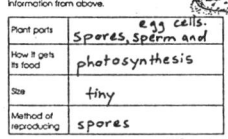

Have you ever seen a smooth, green, velvety carpet growing on a moist forest floor? This carpet is made of hundreds of tiny moss plants growing closely together.

Mosses, like ferns, do not produce seeds; they reproduce with spores. Sperm cells and egg cells are formed at the top of the moss plant. After a rain, the sperm travels through the water to the egg cell. The fertilized egg cell sprouts a tall stalk with a case for the spores at its tip. These spores will produce new mosses. Mosses make their food by photosynthesis, but unlike other green plants, they do not have roots, leaves or stems. Food and water travel slowly from cell to cell.

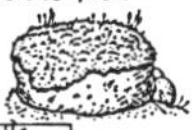

Complete the chart using the information from above.

Plant parts	**egg cells, spores, sperm and**
How it gets its food	**photosynthesis**
Size	**tiny**
Method of reproducing	**spores**

1. Why must mosses live in wet places? **The sperm must travel in water for reproduction.**
2. How are mosses like ferns? **Both reproduce with spores.**
3. How are mosses different from other green plants? **Mosses do not have roots, leaves or stems.**

Fungus Among Us

A fungus plant is not a true plant, because it does not have roots, stems, leaves, or chlorophyll. Fungi cannot make their own food like green plants. Instead, they get their energy by absorbing food from dead or living matter.

Most fungi reproduce by forming spores. The spores fall on dead organisms. A tiny cell breaks out of the spore and grows into fuzzy threads. The threads form new caps, stalks, or capsules.

Fungi are helpful members of nature's recycling team. They help break down dead organisms that can then become part of the soil.

Complete the following sentences using the words in bold.
1. Most fungi reproduce by forming **spores**.
2. Fungi do not have roots, **stems**, or **leaves**.
3. Fungi cannot make their own **food**.
4. Fungi are not green; they lack **chlorophyll**.
5. Mold and mushrooms are types of **fungi**.
6. Fungi break down dead organisms that become part of the **soil**.

Use the numbered letters to solve the riddle.
"What kind of room has no walls, windows, or doors?"
mushroom

Baker's Buddy

Yeast is another kind of fungus. Yeast differs from other fungi in two ways. First, yeast is made of only one cell. Second, yeast can reproduce in two ways. Each cell can grow a small bump, called a bud. When this bud grows large enough, it breaks off and forms a new cell. This is called budding. The second way of reproducing is when the cell divides two or three times inside the cell case. The new cells become spores and stay inside until the case breaks open.

Yeast grows rapidly when it has sugar for food. When yeast breaks down the sugar, it gives off carbon dioxide gas bubbles and alcohol. These bubbles cause bread dough to swell up. Yeast really is a baker's buddy!

Answer the following questions by unscrambling the letters in each yeast cell. The letters will "bud" into the correct answers.
1. Yeast is a kind of **fungus**
2. Yeast is made of only one **cell**
3. Reproducing by making little bumps is called **budding**
4. Yeast divides in the cell case and forms **spores**

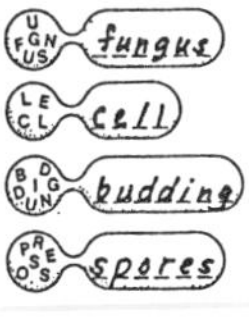

Find Out
Find out what Matzo is. How does it get its name?

© Instructional Fair, Inc.   IF0233 Science Enrichment

Algae

Algae is one of the simplest forms of plant life. Like fungus, algae does not have roots, stems, or leaves. Unlike fungus, algae has chlorophyll and can make its own food by photosynthesis.

Algae can range in size from single cells in your aquarium to the giant Pacific kelp that grows to a length of sixty centimeters!

Complete the chart using the above information.

Size	single cell – 60 cm
How it makes food	photosynthesis
Habitat	any place with water
Plant parts	cells

1. In what ways is algae similar to fungi? **It lacks roots, stems, and leaves.**
2. In what way is algae different than fungi? **It has chlorophyll and makes its food by photosynthesis.**

Find Out
Lichens are some of the plant world's most unusual organisms. Actually, lichens are two organisms – algae and fungi – that live together. Do some research on lichens. Why are lichens so unusual? Could algae and fungi survive alone? Explain.

A World of Plants

Scientists have a special way of classifying, or grouping, the many kinds of plants. Study the diagram below.

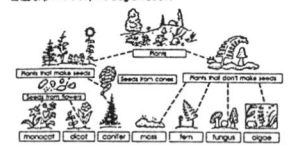

Look carefully at the plant characteristics listed below. Place a (✓) in the column or columns that represent the plant with that characteristic.

	monocot	dicot	conifer	moss	fern	fungus	algae
1. makes seeds	✓	✓	✓				
2. makes seeds in a flower	✓	✓					
3. flower-made seeds with two seed parts		✓					
4. flower-made seeds with one seed part	✓						
5. makes seeds in a cone			✓				
6. produces spores				✓	✓	✓	
7. has leaves with veins		✓					
8. has leaves with parallel veins	✓						
9. has leaves with net-like veins		✓					
10. has needle-like leaves			✓				
11. one-celled plant							✓

Puzzling Plants

Complete the puzzle using words from the Word Bank.

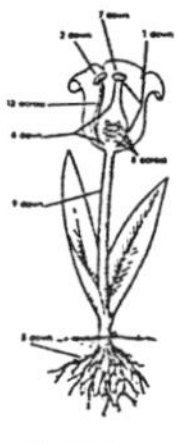

Across
1. Gold dust found in the stamen
3. Makes seeds in a cone
4. Product of photosynthesis
7. Means of reproduction for ferns, molds, and yeast
8. See diagram.
11. Plant's food making process
12. See diagram.

Down
1. See diagram.
2. See diagram.
3. Green coloring in leaves
5. See diagram.
6. See diagram.
7. See diagram.
9. See diagram.
10. Two food parts

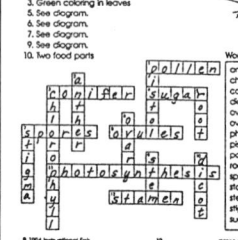

Word Bank
anther
chlorophyll
conifer
dicot
ovary
ovules
photosynthesis
pistil
pollen
root
spores
stamen
stem
stigma
sugar

Classy Creatures

CLASSIFY

Scientists use a special tool to help them find the names of insects, trees, and many other things. It is called a dichotomist key.

Each of the creatures above has a name. We will use our own dichotomist key to give each creature its name. To use the key, work with only one creature at a time. First read steps 1a and 1b. Decide which statement is true about the creature. Then follow the directions after that step. The directions will lead you to a new pair of steps. Keep this up until you come to a step that gives you the creature's name. Write the creature's name in the space provided. After you have named all of the creatures, you will be able to complete the following sentence:

A dichotomist key is used to **classify.**

If this is true . . .	do this:
1 a. The creature has two eyes.	Go to step 2.
b. The creature has one eye.	Go to step 5.
2 a. The creature has one or more antennae.	Go to step 3.
b. The creature has no antennae.	Its name is "L".
3 a. The creature has one antenna.	Its name is "I".
b. The creature has more than one antenna.	Go to step 4.
4 a. The creature has two antennae.	Its name is "S".
b. The creature has three antennae.	Its name is "C".
5 a. The creature has one or more antennae.	Go to step 6.
b. The creature has no antennae.	Its name is "A".
6 a. The creature has one antenna.	Its name is "F".
b. The creature has two antennae.	Its name is "Y".

Backbone or No Backbone

The animal kingdom can be divided into two groups, vertebrates and invertebrates. Vertebrates are animals with backbones. The vertebrae backbone is made of several bones called vertebrae. Each vertebra is separated by a thin disc of cartilage. The backbone supports the body and helps the animal move.

Some invertebrates, like crabs and lobsters, have hard, outer-body coverings. Some invertebrates, like worms, are soft all the way through their bodies.

Circle all of the hidden animals in the puzzle below. Then list them in their own group.

Word Bank
butterfly, skunk, cow, snail, crayfish, snake, deer, spider, dog, swan, fish, wasp, grasshopper, worm

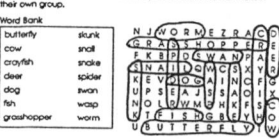

Vertebrates	Invertebrates
cow	butterfly
deer	crayfish
dog	grasshopper
fish	snail
skunk	spider
snake	wasp
swan	worm

Warm- and Cold-Blooded Animals

Mammals and birds are warm-blooded animals. Warm-blooded animals maintain a constant body temperature with the help of hair or feathers as insulation. Warm-blooded animals are called endothermic animals.

Cold-blooded animals, such as fish, reptiles, and amphibians, get their body heat from their surroundings. Their body temperature varies according to the temperature of their environment. Cold-blooded animals are called ectothermic animals.

Circle all of the animals in the wordsearch below. Then list the animals in the proper group.

Word Bank
bear, rat, deer, salamander, duck, shark, eagle, snake, fox, toad, frog, turtle, lizard, owl

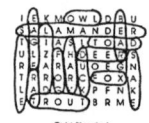

Warm-Blooded

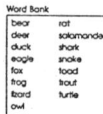

Mammal	Bird
bear	duck
deer	eagle
fox	owl
rat	shark

Cold-Blooded

Fish	Reptile	Amphibian
trout	lizard	frog
	snake	salamander
	turtle	toad

Invertebrates

Just three groups of the many kinds of invertebrates are listed below. The first group are arthropods. Arthropods are invertebrates with jointed legs. Insects, spiders, and crustaceans, like lobsters and crabs, belong to this group. Worms are slender, creeping animals with soft bodies and no legs. The last group are mollusks. Mollusks are soft-bodied, but most have shells for protection. Some mollusks, like the octopus, do not have shells.

Find some examples of invertebrates in the puzzle below. Then list them under the group they belong to.

Word Bank
ant, crayfish, lobster, oyster, squid, clam, earthworm, moth, roundworm, tapeworm, crab, flatworm, octopus, snail

Arthropods	Worms	Mollusks
ant	earthworm	clam
lobster	roundworm	squid
crab	tapeworm	oyster
moth	flatworm	snail
crayfish		octopus

Animals with a Double Life

Amphibians are cold-blooded vertebrates. The word amphibia means to live a double life. Some amphibians live exclusively on land or in the water, while others live in both habitats. Frogs, toads, and salamanders are three of the most common amphibians.

Adult frogs and toads are able to hear you sneak up on them because they have large eardrums, called tympanums. Salamanders do not have eardrums but sense vibrations through their legs.

Frogs and toads develop from eggs that are laid in the water. The larval forms of the frog and toad are called tadpoles. Salamanders hatch from eggs within the adult.

Use the pictures and information above to complete the chart. Make a (✓) in the correct box or boxes.

	Frog	Toad	Salamander
smooth skin	✓		✓
bumpy skin		✓	
nostrils	✓	✓	✓
tympanum	✓	✓	
tail	as tadpole	as tadpole	✓
strong hind legs	✓	✓	
backbone	✓	✓	✓
warm-blooded			
cold-blooded	✓	✓	✓

Food Chains

In the woodland and aquatic communities, there are a large number of food chains. Study the picture on this page.

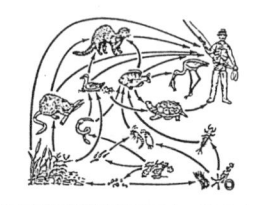

Find at least three food chains in the scene above. List the food chains below.

Food Chain #1	Food Chain #2	Food Chain #3
Possible answers:		
leaves	plants	plants
worm	tadpole	duck
fish	crayfish	man
human	fish	
	otter	

© Instructional Fair, Inc.

IF0233 Science Enrichment

Meat, Salad, and Casseroles

Animals and plants often get their food from different sources. Plants that make their food from sunlight, air, and water are called producers. Animals that are consumers; they get their food from other sources. Animals that eat only plants are called herbivores. Carnivores are animals that eat only meat. Omnivores are animals that eat both plants and meat. Which of these are you?

Study the picture below. Then list all the carnivores, herbivores, omnivores, and producers that you can find.

Carnivore	Herbivore	Omnivore	Producer
snake	rabbit	raccoon	cattail
hawk	butterfly	man	grass
turtle	bird	bird	tree

Food Webs

Most animals, like humans, eat more than one kind of food. This means that most animals are members of more than one food chain. Separate food chains that interlock are called food webs.

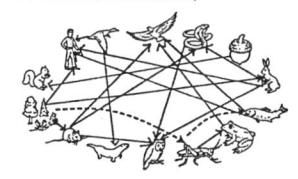

Form a food web by drawing arrows from each prey to its predator. Remember - most prey have more than one predator. (Hint: Use a different colored crayon for each food chain.)

One food chain that you may have found in the food web is this one:
plant → grasshopper → trout → otter
Answers will vary.

Write one more food chain that you found in your food web.
plant → mouse → snake → owl
plant → rabbit → human

Gone for the Winter

When the cold winds blow, some animals travel to other regions for the winter. In the spring, they travel back to their summer habitat. This movement is called migration. Some animals migrate to warmer climates to find food. Others, like salmon and whales, migrate to give birth to their young.

Below are three pictures of migration. Choose one of the pictures and write a brief news article for the outdoor section of your newspaper. Use the five W's (who, what, where, when, and why) in your article.

Articles will vary.

Endangered

Today, thousands of animals are in danger of becoming extinct. The jaguar, polar bear, sperm whale, and African elephant are only a few of the many animals that people have endangered. These animals are hunted for meat, fur, and trophies.

Some animals are endangered because their habitats are being destroyed by land development.

Most recently, man has polluted the environment with pesticides and fertilizers that have poisoned the food of many animals. Insecticides have entered the bald eagle's food chain, causing the now thin-shelled eggs to break before hatching.

Use another source to find out the names of other animals that are endangered or extinct. Then fill in the chart below.

Animal	Endangered or Extinct	Why?
		Some endangered animals for research: whooping crane, California condor, bald eagle, wood bison, Key deer, American alligator, giant panda

The Tortoise and the Hare

Many animals depend on their speed to escape from predators. Other animals use their speed to capture prey. Graph the speeds of these animals on the chart below from slowest to fastest. Then answer the questions below.

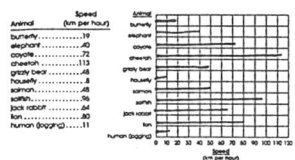

Animal	Speed (km per hour)
butterfly	19
elephant	40
coyote	72
cheetah	113
grizzly bear	48
housefly	8
salmon	48
sailfish	96
jack rabbit	64
lion	80
human (jogging)	11

Both the coyote and the rabbit are very fast animals, but each uses its speed in a different way. How does each animal use its speed?
A coyote chases its prey. A rabbit runs from its enemies.

The tortoise is not very fast, but it has other adaptations to aid in protection. How does the tortoise protect itself?
It uses its hard shell.

Animal Facts

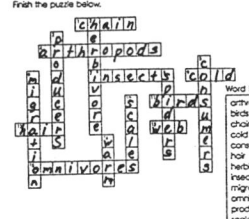

Finish the puzzle below.

Word Bank: arthropods, birds, chain, cold, consumers, hair, herbivore, insects, migration, omnivores, producers, scales, spiders, warm, web

Across
1. A series of animals that feed on each other is a ___
4. Invertebrates with jointed legs
7. Largest group of invertebrates
9. Reptiles are ___-blooded.
11. Feathered, warm-blooded vertebrates
12. Body covering of mammals
13. Interlocking food chains form a food ___
15. Organisms that eat both plants and animals

Down
2. Animal that eats only plants
3. Organisms that make their own food
5. Organisms that do not make their own food
6. Seasonal movement of animals
8. Arthropods with eight legs, two body sections, and no antennae
10. Body covering of reptiles
14. Birds and mammals are ___-blooded animals.

"Dem Bones, Dem Dry Bones"

Use your science book or another source to help. Label the skeletal system with the scientific name for each bone.

Scientific Names
a. pelvis
b. vertebrae
c. scapula
d. cranium
e. radius
f. femur
g. mandible
h. tibia
i. patella
j. clavicle
k. coccyx
l. rib

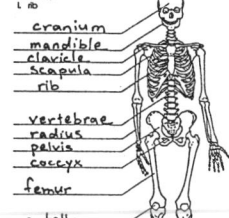

cranium
mandible
clavicle
scapula
rib
vertebrae
radius
pelvis
coccyx
femur
patella
tibia

Muscle Power

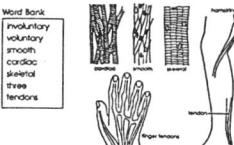

Use your science book or another source to help. Fill in the blanks with words from the Word Bank.

Word Bank: involuntary, voluntary, smooth, cardiac, skeletal, three, tendons

There are **three** kinds of muscles. Internal organs, such as the intestines, the stomach, and the esophagus are moved by the **smooth** muscles. The **skeletal** muscles move your skeleton and external body parts. The heart muscle is controlled by the **cardiac** muscle. Muscles which need a special message from your brain in order to work are called **voluntary** muscles. Muscles which move automatically, without conscious thought, are called **involuntary** muscles. The tough cords that connect the skeletal muscles to your bones are called **tendons**.

Message Transmissions

Use your science book or another source to help. Fill in the spaces with words from the Word Bank.

Your body has its own system for sending messages to your brain. This system of individual nerves and their pathways is found throughout the body. It is called the peripheral nervous system. The peripheral nervous system is a pathway to the brain for your five senses. It also serves your internal organs and helps you respond to your environment.

Word Bank: axons, dendrites, synapse, neurons

Messages are sent to the brain through a network of nerve cells called **neurons**. Neurons have longs arms, called **axons**, and shorter arms, called **dendrites**.

In order for messages to travel along the pathway, the neurons must connect with each other. This connection is called a **synapse**.

Messages enter each neuron through the dendrite. Messages exit the neuron through the axon.

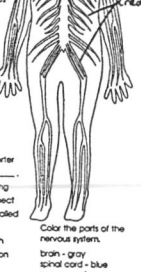

Color the parts of the nervous system.
brain - gray
spinal cord - blue
nerves - red

© Instructional Fair, Inc.

IF0233 Science Enrichment

Think Fast

While riding your bike down the street, a car suddenly pulls out in front of you. Your eyes send a message to your brain. Your brain sends a message to your arteries. You can feel your brakes. How long did it take you to stop? This time is called your reaction time.

Here is a simple experiment to find out your reaction time. The only materials you will need are a 30 cm ruler and a partner.

1. Place your left arm on your desk with your hand over the edge.
2. Space your thumb and index finger apart a little more than the thickness of the ruler.
3. Your partner will hold one end of the ruler with the other end level with the top of your index finger.
4. Your partner will say "ready," pause a few seconds, and drop the ruler.
5. Catch the ruler and check the distance by reading the level at the bottom of the index finger.
6. Record your results.
7. Now, try the experiment again with your right hand.

Trial	Left hand	Right hand
1		
2	Answers will	
3	vary.	
4		
5		

Average: _____

Which hand had the fastest reaction time?

Fun Fact
Nerve impulses, or messages, travel at 100 meters per second!

Interbody Highway System

Veins, arteries, and capillaries are the blood vessels that form the fantastic highway system in your body.

Write vein, artery, or capillary in front of the statement that best describes the type of blood vessel.

1. **artery** carries blood away from the heart.
2. **vein** carries blood back to the heart.
3. **capillary** is the tiniest blood vessel.
4. **artery** carries oxygen-rich blood.
5. **capillary** connects the veins and arteries.

Your blood is the vehicle that travels this highway. It transports oxygen, carbon dioxide, food, and waste. Your blood also fights infection and clots to prevent excessive blood loss.

Team Work

Your heart is really two pumps that work together like a team. The right side of your heart takes dirty, carbon dioxide-filled blood in through the right atrium and right ventricle. It then pumps it through the pulmonary artery into your lungs. The blood is filled with oxygen and passes through the pulmonary vein and into the left atrium and left ventricle on the left side of the heart. The left side of the heart then pumps this rich, oxygen-filled blood through the main artery of the body, called the aorta, to all the parts of your body.

Use arrows to trace the path of the blood.
Color the part of the heart filled with dirty, carbon dioxide-filled blood in blue.
Color the areas filled with oxygen-rich blood in red.

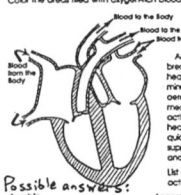

Activities that make you breathe deeply and your heart beat faster for 5 minutes or more are called aerobic activities. Aerobic means "using oxygen." These activities help strengthen your heart. Activities that are done quickly and don't require new supplies of oxygen are called anaerobic activities.

List aerobic and anaerobic activities that you enjoy.

Possible answers:
Aerobic
1. jogging
2. soccer
3. swimming
4. bicycling
5. skating

Anaerobic
1. quick, short races
2. baseball
3. bowling
4. reading
5. playing checkers

Pick Up the Beat

Your pulse is caused by the stopping and starting of the blood as it rushes through your arteries. You can feel your pulse at any spot on an artery is near the surface of the skin. These spots are called pulse points. One pulse point is located on the inside of your wrist.

Name some other pulse points.
ankles
biceps
side of neck

Your pulse rate changes during different kinds of activity. Check your pulse rate after doing these activities.

Activity	Pulse rate for 15 seconds	Multiply by 4	Pulse rate for 1 minute
sitting			
hopping 25 times	Answers will vary.		
hopping 100 times			
lying down			

How does your pulse rate change during exercise?
It increases.

Why do you think your pulse rate changes during exercise?
As muscles need oxygen your heart pumps faster.

Respiratory System

Your breathing, or respiratory, system is made of many parts. Solve the respiratory riddles using the Word Bank.

1. "I'm the windpipe that brings fresh air to your lungs."
   trachea

2. "There are 600 million of us tiny air sacs in your lungs."
   alveoli

3. "Tra-la-la. I'm your voice box."
   larynx

4. "We branch to the left and right from your windpipe."
   bronchial tubes

5. "I enter your lungs with each breath of fresh air."
   oxygen

6. "I help squeeze the air out of your lungs."
   diaphragm

Label the diagram using the words from the Word Bank.

Word Bank
alveoli
bronchial tubes
diaphragm
larynx
oxygen
trachea

Labels: larynx, trachea, bronchial tubes, alveoli, diaphragm

Digestive System

Use your science book and the Word Bank to help label the parts of the digestive system.

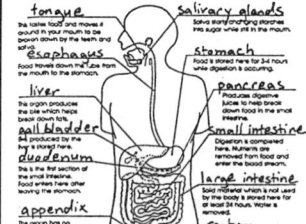

tongue - The saliva ''uses'' and moves it around in your mouth to be gnawed down by the teeth and saliva.

esophagus - Food travels down the tube which helps take it from the mouth to the stomach.

liver - This organ produces the bile which helps break down fats.

gall bladder - Bile produced by the liver is stored here.

duodenum - This is the first section of the small intestine. Food enters here after leaving the stomach.

appendix - This organ has no function.

salivary glands - Saliva starts changing starches into sugar while still in the mouth.

stomach - Food is stored here for 3-4 hours while digestion is occurring.

pancreas - Produces digestive juices to help break down food in the small intestine.

small intestine - Digestion is completed here. Nutrients are removed from food and enter the bowel stream.

large intestine - Solid material which is not used by the body is stored here for at least 24 hours. Water is removed.

rectum - Waste (solid material) which has not been digested is stored here until ready to exit the body.

anus - Waste exits through the body opening.

Word Bank
pancreas   duodenum
stomach   small intestine
liver   salivary glands
appendix   gall bladder
tongue   rectum
large intestine   anus
esophagus

Keep It Covered

Your skin does more than cover your body. Your skin does three important jobs. It helps keep your body cool and comfortable. It is a sensor that warns you of danger. And it provides protection from dirt and bacteria.

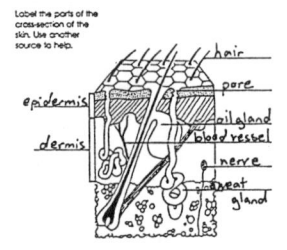

Label the parts of the cross-section of the skin. Use another source to help.

Labels: hair, pore, epidermis, oil gland, dermis, blood vessel, nerve, sweat gland

How does your skin help you in the following situations?
heat **Sweat glands help keep your body cool.**
dirt **Skin keeps out dirt and bacteria.**
pain **Nerves send pain messages causing you to react and avoid injury.**

The Body's Camera

Use your science book or another source to help. Label the parts of the eye with terms from the Word Bank.

Word Bank
lens   optic nerve   pupil   sclera
cornea iris   retina   vitreous humor

Labels: optic nerve, retina, lens, cornea, vitreous humor, pupil, iris, sclera

Something Special
Your retina is made up of light-sensitive cells that can be stimulated by pressure. Close your eyes and very gently press on them. The stars that you are seeing are called pressure flashes.

Catching Good Vibes

Use your science book or another source to help. Complete the following sentences using the Word Bank.

The ear honks its horn. The sound waves are collected by your **auricle** and travel down the **auditory canal**. The sound strikes the **ear drum** causing the tight skin to vibrate. Three tiny bones called the **hammer**, **anvil**, and **stirrup** magnify and send the sound to the inner ear. The sound travels to the **cochlea**, a coiled, snail-shaped passage filled with liquid and nerve hairs. The nerve hairs send signals through the **auditory nerve** to the brain.

Label the parts of the ear using the Word Bank.

1) hammer
2) anvil
3) stirrup
auditory nerve
cochlea
eardrum
auditory canal

Word Bank
auricle
ear drum
auditory canal
auditory nerve
hammer
anvil
stirrup
cochlea

© Instructional Fair, Inc.   IF0233 Science Enrichment

Joe's Tooth: The Inside Story

Use your science book or another source to help.

Word Bank
| neck | crown | enamel | dentin |
| root | cementum | pulp | |

Label the inside parts of Joe's tooth using the Word Bank.
Label the outside parts of Joe's tooth using the Word Bank.

- enamel
- dentin
- pulp
- cementum
- crown
- neck
- root

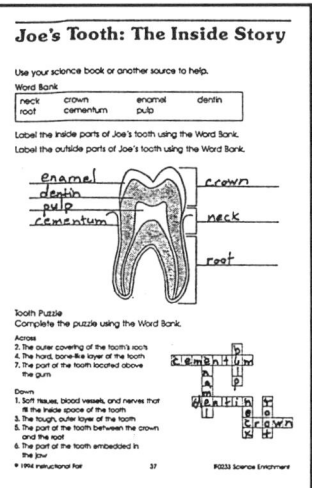

Tooth Puzzle
Complete the puzzle using the Word Bank.

Across
2. The outer covering of the tooth's root
4. The hard, bone-like layer of the tooth
7. The part of the tooth located above the gum

Down
1. Soft tissues, blood vessels, and nerves that fill the inside space of the tooth
3. The tough, outer layer of the tooth
5. The part of the tooth between the crown and the root
6. The part of the tooth embedded in the jaw

Crossword answers: cementum, dentin, enamel, crown

Nibblers and Chompers

Use your science book or another source to help.
Fill in the spaces with words from the Word Bank.

You have four kinds of __teeth__ in your mouth, each with a special job. The large, front teeth are called __incisors__. The incisors are the nippers that help you bite into an apple. The sharp pointy teeth are __canines__. Canines are used to tear food, like when you chew meat off a bone. The __bicuspids__ are large teeth with two points. The __molars__ are the large, flat teeth in the back of your mouth. Both the bicuspids and molars are the "millstones" used for grinding food.

Label the teeth on the diagram by printing the following letters on the teeth:
I = Incisors C = Canines B = Bicuspids M = Molars

Word Bank
- canines
- bicuspids
- incisors
- molars
- teeth

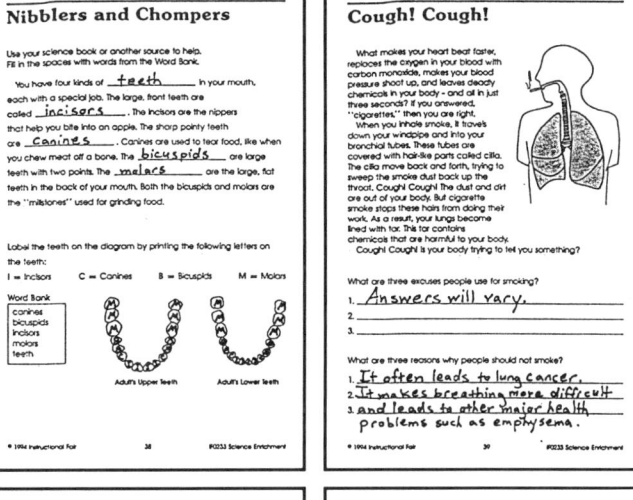

Adult's Upper Teeth   Adult's Lower Teeth

Cough! Cough!

What makes your heart beat faster, replaces the oxygen in your blood with carbon monoxide, makes your blood pressure shoot up, and leaves deadly chemicals in your body – and all in just three seconds? If you answered, "cigarettes," then you are right.

When you inhale smoke, it travels down your windpipe and into your bronchial tubes. These tubes are covered with hair-like parts called cilia. The cilia move back and forth, trying to sweep the smoke dust back up the throat. Cough! Cough! The dust and dirt are out of your body. But cigarette smoke stops these hairs from doing their work. As a result, your lungs become lined with tar. This tar contains chemicals that are harmful to your body. Cough! Cough! is your body trying to tell you something?

What are three excuses people use for smoking?
1. __Answers will vary.__
2. _____
3. _____

What are three reasons why people should not smoke?
1. __It often leads to lung cancer.__
2. __It makes breathing more difficult__
3. __and leads to other major health problems such as emphysema.__

Body Trivia

Test your knowledge of the human body with these amazing facts.

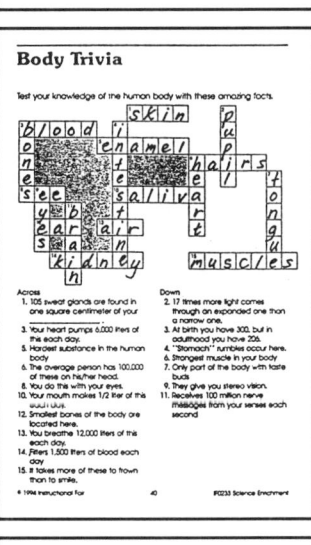

Crossword with words: skin, blood, enamel, hairs, see, saliva, ear, muscles, kidney, etc.

Across
1. 105 sweat glands are found in one square centimeter of your ___.
3. Your heart pumps 6,000 liters of this each day.
5. Hardest substance in the human body
6. The average person has 100,000 of these on his/her head.
8. You do this with your eyes.
10. Your mouth makes 1/2 liter of this each day.
12. Smallest bones of the body are located here.
13. You breathe 12,000 liters of this each day.
14. Filters 1,500 liters of blood each day
15. It takes more of these to frown than to smile.

Down
2. 17 times more light comes through an expanded one than a narrow one.
4. At birth you have 300, but in adulthood you have 206.
6. "Stomach" rumbles occur here.
7. Strongest muscle in your body
9. Only part of the body with taste buds
10. They give you stereo vision.
11. Receives 100 million nerve messages from your senses each second

---

Solid to the Core?

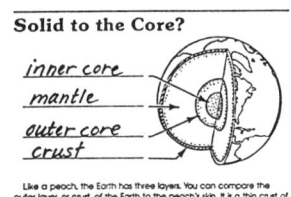

Labels: inner core, mantle, outer core, crust

Like a peach, the Earth has three layers. You can compare the outer layer, or crust, of the Earth to the peach's skin. It is a thin crust of hard rock, from 5 to 70 kilometers thick.
Beneath the crust is the mantle. Like the fleshy part of the peach, it is the thickest layer. The mantle is made of very hot rock that is not liquid, but plastic-like and soft. The mantle is almost 3,000 kilometers thick.
The innermost layer of the earth, the core, is like the peach's pit. The outer core is liquid and most likely made of iron. The outer core is about 2,000 kilometers thick. The inner core is solid and seems to be made of iron and nickel. The inner core is 1,500 kilometers thick.

- Use the words in bold above to label the diagram of the Earth.

1. How far is it from the surface to the center of the Earth? __6,570 kilometers__
2. The Earth's crust is __5 to 70__ kilometers thick.
3. The inner core is made from iron and __nickel__.
4. The outer core is made of __iron__.
5. The innermost layer of the Earth is called the __core__.

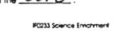

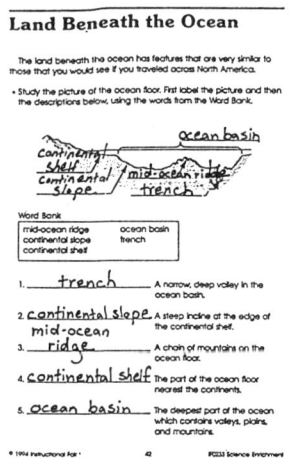

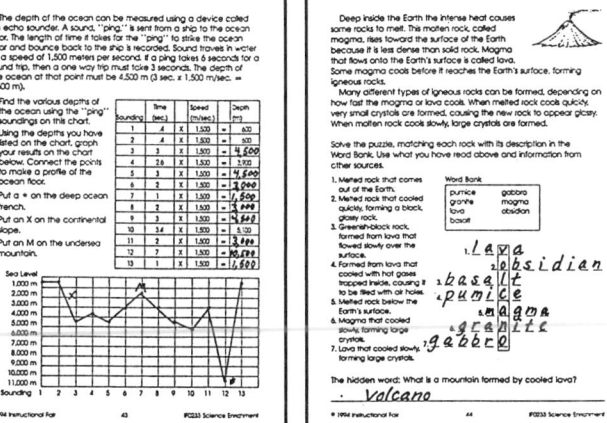

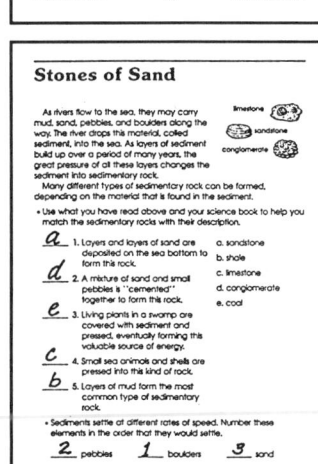

Land Beneath the Ocean

The land beneath the ocean has features that are very similar to those that you would see if you traveled across North America.

- Study the picture of the ocean floor. First label the picture and then the descriptions below, using the words from the Word Bank.

Labels: continental shelf, continental slope, ocean basin, mid-ocean ridge, trench

Word Bank
- mid-ocean ridge
- continental slope
- continental shelf
- ocean basin
- trench

1. __trench__ — A narrow, deep valley in the ocean basin.
2. __continental slope__ — A steep incline at the edge of the continental shelf.
   __mid-ocean ridge__
3. __ridge__ — A chain of mountains on the ocean floor.
4. __continental shelf__ — The part of the ocean floor nearest the continents.
5. __ocean basin__ — The deepest part of the ocean which contains valleys, plains, and mountains.

"Ping-Ping"

The depth of the ocean can be measured using a device called an echo sounder. A sound, "ping," is sent from a ship to the ocean floor. The length of time it takes for the "ping" to strike the ocean floor and bounce back to the ship is recorded. Sound travels in water at a speed of 1,500 meters per second. If a ping takes 6 seconds for a round trip, then a one way trip must be 3 seconds. The depth of the ocean at that point must be 4,500 m (3 sec. x 1,500 m/sec. = 4,500 m).

1. Find the various depths of the ocean using the "ping" soundings on this chart.
2. Using the depths you have listed on the chart, graph your results on the chart below. Connect the points to make a profile of the ocean floor.
3. Put a ● on the deep ocean trench.
4. Put an X on the continental slope.
5. Put an M on the undersea mountain.

Sounding	Time (sec.)	Speed (m/sec.)	Depth (m)
1	4	1,500	620
2	4	1,500	620
3	3	1,500	4,500
4	2.6	1,500	3,900
5	3	1,500	4,500
6	2	1,500	3,000
7	1	1,500	1,500
8	2	1,500	3,000
9	3	1,500	4,500
10	3.4	1,500	5,100
11	2	1,500	3,000
12	7	1,500	10,500
13	1	1,500	1,500

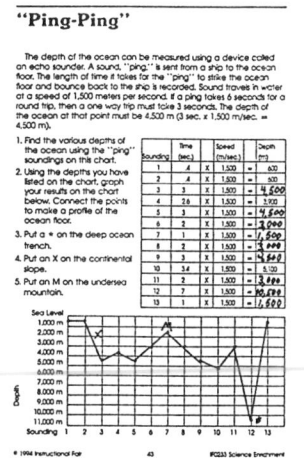

Fire Rocks

Deep inside the Earth the intense heat causes some rocks to melt. This molten rock, called magma, rises toward the surface of the Earth because it is less dense than solid rock. Magma that cools beneath the Earth's surface is called igneous rocks.
Some magma cools before it reaches the Earth's surface, forming igneous rocks.
Many different types of igneous rocks can be formed, depending on how fast the magma or lava cools. When melted rock cools quickly, very small crystals are formed, causing the new rock to appear glassy. When molten rock cools slowly, large crystals are formed.

Solve the puzzle, matching each rock with its description in the Word Bank. Use what you have read above and information from other sources.

1. Melted rock that comes out of the Earth.
2. Melted rock that cooled quickly, forming a black, glassy rock.
3. Greenish-black rock, formed from lava that flowed slowly over the surface.
4. Formed from lava that cooled with hot gases trapped inside, causing it to be filled with air holes.
5. Melted rock below the Earth's surface.
6. Magma that cooled slowly, forming large crystals.
7. Lava that cooled slowly, forming large crystals.

Word Bank
- pumice
- granite
- lava
- basalt
- gabbro
- magma
- obsidian

1. lava
2. obsidian
3. basalt
4. pumice
5. magma
6. granite
7. gabbro

The hidden word: What is a mountain formed by cooled lava? __volcano__

Stones of Sand

As rivers flow to the sea, they may carry mud, sand, pebbles, and boulders along the way. The river drops this material, called sediment, into the sea. As layers of sediment build up over a period of many years, the great pressure of all these layers changes the sediment into sedimentary rock.
Many different types of sedimentary rock can be formed, depending on the material that is found in the sediment.

- Use what you have read above and your science book to help you match the sedimentary rocks with their description.

__a__ 1. Layers and layers of sand are deposited on the sea bottom to form this rock.
__d__ 2. A mixture of sand and small pebbles is "cemented" together to form this rock.
__e__ 3. Living plants in a swamp are covered with sediment and pressed, eventually forming this valuable source of energy.
__c__ 4. Small sea animals and shells are pressed into this kind of rock.
__b__ 5. Layers of mud form the most common type of sedimentary rock.

a. sandstone
b. shale
c. limestone
d. conglomerate
e. coal

- Sediments settle at different rates of speed. Number these elements in the order that they would settle.

__2__ pebbles __1__ boulders __3__ sand

© Instructional Fair, Inc.   IF0233 Science Enrichment

Changing Rocks

With enough pressure and heat, sedimentary and igneous rock can be changed into a new rock. This new kind of rock is called metamorphic, which means "changed in form."

There are a number of ways that metamorphic rock can be formed. One way is when rocks that are buried deep under the Earth's surface are flattened by the great pressure from above them. An example of this is when granite is changed into gneiss. Look carefully at the pictures. How has the appearance of the granite changed?

Rock Cycle

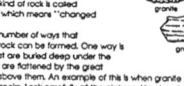

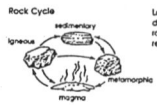

Look closely at the rock cycle diagram. This cycle shows how rock material is mixed and re-used again and again.

Unscramble the terms to show examples of how igneous and sedimentary rocks can change into metamorphic rock.

1. S H A L E changes into S L A T E
   H E S A L   T A L E S
2. G R A N I T E changes into G N E I S S
   T R I N E G A   S I N E G S
3. L I M E S T O N E changes
   M O E S T E L N I
   into M A R B L E
        B E L M A R

Testing Minerals

All minerals have certain characteristics, or properties, which distinguish them from other minerals. Minerals can be identified by the testing of these properties. A scratch test is used to determine the property of hardness. Minerals are rated on a scale of one to ten - one is the softest and ten the hardest.

It usually takes more than one property to identify a mineral, but let's try our skill using the hardness test.

Hardness Number	Test	Mineral
1	Fingernail scratches it easily	talc
2	Fingernail barely scratches it	gypsum/kaolinite
3	Copper penny scratches it	calcite/mica
4	Glass scratches it easily	fluorite
5	Steel knife will scratch it easily	apatite/hornblend
6	It will scratch glass	feldspar
7	It will scratch a steel knife	quartz
8	It will scratch a steel file	topaz
9	It will scratch topaz	corundum
10	It will scratch corundum	diamond

1. It will scratch glass (glassy, colorless). **quartz**
2. Copper penny scratches it (pearly, colorless). **calcite**
3. Copper penny scratches it (pearly, black). **mica**
4. Fingernail barely scratches it (glassy, gray). **gypsum**
5. It will scratch glass (glassy, gray). **feldspar**
6. Fingernail barely scratches it (dull, yellow). **kaolinite**
7. Steel knife will scratch it (glassy, black). **hornblend**
8. Fingernail scratches it easily (pearly, white). **talc**

It's California's Fault!

There are many cracks in the Earth's bedrock. These cracks are called faults. One kind of fault is called a strike-slip fault. The rock along one side of the fault moves horizontally in one direction, while the facing rock moves in the opposite direction. Other times, the bedrock on one side of the fault moves upward, while the other side moves down. This is called a dip-slip fault. The San Andreas Fault is a large strike-slip fault that runs along the coast of California. This famous fault and other smaller faults that form the San Andreas Fault System have been the source of many earthquakes.

1. Label the two types of faults using the words in bold above.
   strike-slip fault   **dip-slip fault**
2. On which side of the San Andreas Fault is San Francisco?
   east
3. On which side of the San Andreas Fault is Santa Cruz?
   west
4. The San Andreas Fault's movement has been measured to be as much as 5 cm per year. What might happen to these two cities a million years from now?
   If they are not destroyed, they might be neighbors.

Ring of Fire

Deep inside the Earth, melted rock called magma moves toward the Earth's surface. When the magma reaches the surface, it is called lava.

In a volcano, the magma travels through a tube-like passageway called a conduit, until it reaches an opening in the Earth's surface, called a vent. The vent may be in the top of the mountain or it could be a side vent. Sometimes the lava flows out gently, but other times it may explode.

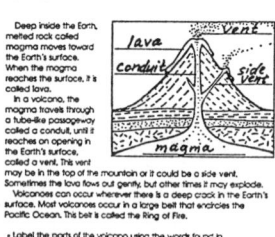

Volcanoes can occur wherever there is a deep crack in the Earth's surface. Most volcanoes occur in a large belt that encircles the Pacific Ocean. This belt is called the Ring of Fire.

- Label the parts of the volcano using the words found in bold above.
- Fill in the blanks to show the types of material that come out of a volcano.

1. Rocks with sharp corners that are blown out from the inside of the volcano. **blocks**
2. Lava blown into the air, cools into small coarse pieces of rock which are puffed up by gas. **cinder**
3. Magma that has reached the surface. **lava**

Word Bank: blocks   cinder   lava

Shake, Rattle, and Roll!

An earthquake is a movement in the Earth's crust. The large blocks of rock along a fault (a crack in the earth) slip past each other. As the blocks of rock slide, their sides may become locked. The strain builds and then becomes too great, causing the rocks to quickly slip past each other. The result is an earthquake. From the origin of the earthquake, called the focus, waves, or vibrations, move out in all directions.

Earthquakes are recorded on a sensitive instrument called a seismograph. The strength of the earthquake is measured on a scale of 1 to 10, with 10 being the strongest. This scale is called the Richter Scale.

Mexico City	2,600 km
Denver	1,400 km
Vancouver	1,600 km

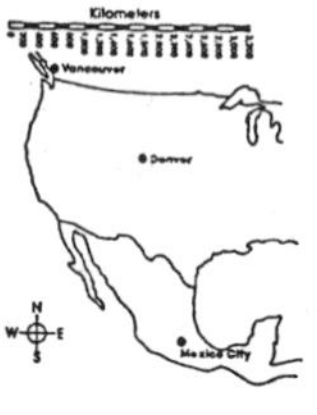

- Seismographs in three cities were able to record the same earthquake. The data showed that the focus of the earthquake was located at different distances from each of the cities. For each city, set your compass for the distance indicated. Draw a circle using the city as its center. Mark the focus by placing an X on the map where the three circles meet.

1. Where do earthquakes usually occur? **along faults**
2. Why might some earthquakes be stronger than others? **blocks. Greater tension or strain between**

Mountain Building

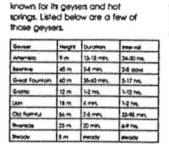

fault-block mountains   **dome mountain**   **folded mountain**

Mammoth mountains can be found in many places throughout the world. How are these mountains formed?

Most mountains are formed when continental plates collide with each other. The force of the plates pushing against each other causes the crust to bulge up higher and higher, until "waves" of mountains are formed. The mountains that are formed this way are called folded mountains.

Other mountains are formed along faults. Along one side of the fault, the block of crust moves up. Along the other side of the fault, the block of crust moves down. The mountains that are formed from this are called fault-block mountains.

A third type of mountain, formed much in the same way folded mountains are, is a dome mountain. A bulge is formed. However, the bulge is caused by magma from the earth's mantle pushing against the crust.

1. Label the drawings of mountain types using the words in bold.
2. What is the main difference between a folded mountain and a fault-block mountain?
   The fault-block is forced up by the shifting of blocks of crust along a fault; the folded is forced up by pushing plates.
3. What are two forces that form mountains?
   1. **force of moving plates**
   2. **force of magma pushing up**

Natural Fountains

Geysers, those spectacular natural fountains of spurting hot water, are actually a special kind of hot spring.

Water from rain and snow seeps thousands of meters underground. There the water is heated to 204°F or higher, a temperature far above the boiling point of water. This superheated water expands and rises to the surface, where the steam bubbles escape. But from time to time, the bubbles become too abundant to pass up through the water. When this happens, so much steam builds up that the water actually explodes out of a vent in the ground, rising anywhere from 1 m to 60 m into the air. Yellowstone National Park is known for its geysers and hot springs. Listed below are a few of those geysers.

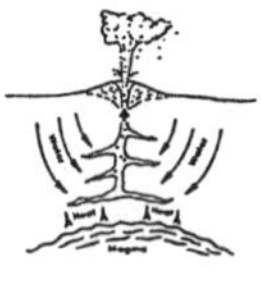

Geyser	Height	Duration	Interval
Aremica	1 m	13-15 min	26-30 min
Beehive	45 m	5-6 min	24 pers
Great Fountain	40 m	35-60 min	5-17 hr
Giante	1/2 m	1-2 min	1-12 hr
Lion	18 m	4 min	1-2 hr
Old Faithful	34 m	4 min	1-12 hr
Riverside	23 m	20 min	6-7 hr
Steady	1 m	steady	steady

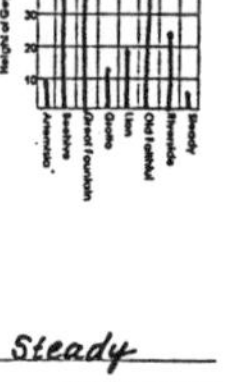

1. Graph the height of each geyser.
2. Which geyser erupts the most often? **Steady**

Rivers of Ice

A large mass of snow and ice that lasts for years and years is called a glacier. Glaciers form over a period of years when more snow falls in the winter than melts in the summer. As the snow accumulates, the snow deep under the surface shows compression into thick, dense ice. The ice, called firn, can be from 30 to 50 meters thick.

In mountainous regions, the downward pull of gravity on the ice causes the flow down the mountainside. As the glacier flows, it picks up rocks and stones. When the glacier melts, the rocks and stones are deposited in small mounds called moraines.

- The force of a glacier has left these glacial terms in a bit of a mess. Unscramble them. You may consult your science book or another resource book.

Glacier formed long smooth hill. **DRUMLINS**
                                  DMLRUNIS

Refrozen snowmelt in a glacier. **FIRN**
                                 FNIR

Large crack in a glacier. **CREVASSE**
                           SRACESEV

Melted glacial ice. **MELTWATER**
                     MTWTEALER

Small mound formed by the deposit of rocks from a melting glacier. **MORAINE**
                                                                    ROMINAE

Just Plain Dirt

Soil is made of pieces of rocks and minerals that have been broken down by nature over a period of thousands of years.
Soil is found in three layers. The top layer, where plants usually grow, is called topsoil. The second layer, which contains pebbles, sand, and clay, is called subsoil. The bottom layer contains large rocks and is called bedrock.

- How is soil formed? **Rocks and minerals are broken down by rain, snow, wind, or other forces of nature.**
- The foundation of a very large building often goes all the way down to the bedrock. Why? **Bedrock provides a stable base, below shifting topsoil and subsoil, on which to secure the weight of heavy buildings.**

Soil	Structure	Properties
Sand	Small pieces of quartz	Does not hold water
Clay	Very small pieces of mineral other than quartz	Holds water very well
Loam	Sand, clay, and humus (decayed plants and animals)	Holds water yet drains

Tell what type of soil you would choose in each situation below. The chart will help you.

1. Garden **loam** Why? **It both holds and drains water. The humus component provides nutrition.**
2. Bottom of a manmade pond **clay** Why? **It holds water and may prevent leakage.**

Earth Shattering Review

Down
1. Small mound formed by a deposit of rocks from a glacier.
3. Movement in the Earth's crust caused by the slipping of large blocks of rock along a fault.
6. Rocks formed by layers of sediment under great pressure.
8. Remains or imprints of organisms left in sedimentary rock.
9. A narrow, deep valley in the ocean basin.

Across
2. Rocks that are changed in form.
4. The thin outer layer of the Earth.
5. Rocks formed by the cooling of magma.
7. The innermost layer of the Earth.
8. A crack in the Earth's surface.
10. Molten rock beneath the surface of the Earth.
11. Layer of rock between the Earth's core and crust.

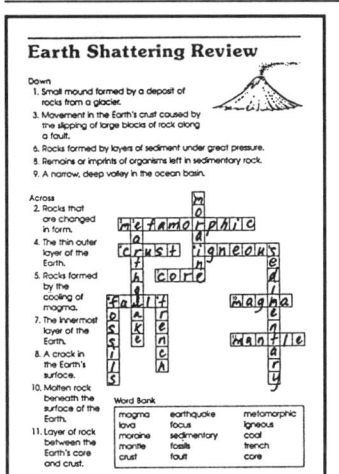

Across answers filled in: metamorphic, crust, igneous, core, fault, magma, mantle

Word Bank
magma, earthquake, metamorphic, lava, focus, igneous, moraine, sedimentary, coal, mantle, fossils, trench, crust, fault, core

Our Moon

On July 20, 1969, Neil Armstrong and Edwin Aldrin left the first footprints on the moon. The astronauts found our moon to be without air, water, plants, or any living things.

The moon is covered with billions of bowl-shaped holes called craters. Scientists believe the craters were formed when objects traveling in space hit and dented the moon's surface.

When you look at the moon with a telescope, you will see large, flat, smoother areas. Early astronomers believed that these areas were oceans. They called the areas maria, which means "seas" in Latin. Actually, there is no water on the moon. Maria are dry lava beds that were formed by volcanic action on the moon about 3½ million years ago.

Pretend you are an astronaut preparing for a visit to the moon. Decide which items from the list below would be needed or not needed for your visit. Give your reasons.

Item	Needed	Not Needed	Reason
signal whistle		✓	without air, sound does not travel
matches		✓	no oxygen for combustion
water	✓		no water available
raincoat		✓	no rain
lightweight equipment		✓	moon's gravity ⅙ of Earth
oxygen	✓		no oxygen
food	✓		no food

Changing Faces

Have you ever noticed that the moon's face appears to have different shapes at different times of the month? These changes in shape are called the moon's phases. Of course, the moon does not actually change shape, nor does it produce its own light. Do you know what accounts for the moon's shape and light?

As the moon revolves around the Earth, we can see different amounts of the moon's lighted part. Study the drawing of the moon's different phases carefully.

a) Gibbous — Half
b) Crescent
3) Full — c) Planet
d) New
e) Gibbous — f) Crescent
Half

Draw each of the moon's phases as seen from Earth. Label each phase.

1. New 2. Waxing Crescent 3. Waxing Half 4. Waxing Gibbous
5. Full 6. Waning Gibbous 7. Waning Half 8. Waning Crescent

Space Shadows

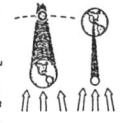

Objects in space often cast shadows. Sometimes the moon passes between the Earth and the sun. The moon slowly blocks out the sun's light, casting a shadow on the Earth. The sky gets dark, the air cools, and for several minutes you can see the stars. This is a solar eclipse.

As the moon travels around the Earth, sometimes the Earth will cast a shadow on the moon. The full moon darkens as it moves into the Earth's shadow. This eclipse, which will last for over an hour, is called a lunar eclipse.

Draw the position of the moon and the shadows for both the solar and lunar eclipses. Label each picture.

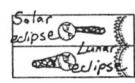

Solar eclipse / Lunar eclipse

Complete the following chart by checking the correct box for each statement.

	Lunar Eclipse	Solar Eclipse
Earth casts a shadow	✓	
moon casts a shadow		✓
takes place at night	✓	
takes place during the day		✓
moon is blocked out	✓	
sun's blocked out		✓
causes the sky to get dark		✓
causes the air to cool		✓

Exploring Our Solar System

You can learn much about the planets in our Solar System by studying the table on this page. Use the information from the table to answer the questions.

Planet	Diameter	Distance from the Sun	Revolution	Rotation
Mercury	4,880 km	57,900,000 km	88 days	59 days
Venus	12,100 km	108,200,000 km	225 days	243 days
Earth	12,756 km	149,600,000 km	365 days	24 hours
Mars	6,794 km	228,000,000 km	687 days	24.5 hours
Jupiter	143,200 km	778,400,000 km	11.9 years	10 hours
Saturn	120,000 km	1,425,600,000 km	29.5 years	11 hours
Uranus	51,800 km	2,867,000,000 km	84 years	16 hours
Neptune	49,500 km	4,456,000,000 km	164 years	18.5 hours
Pluto	2,600 km	5,890,000,000 km	247 years	6.5 days

1. Which planet is closest to the sun? **Mercury**
2. Which planet is farthest from the sun? **Pluto**
3. Which planets are located between Earth and the sun? **Venus and Mercury**
4. Which is the largest planet? **Jupiter**
5. Which is the smallest planet? **Pluto**
6. What is the diameter of Earth? **12,756 km**
7. How long does it take for Pluto to revolve around the sun? **247 years**
8. Which planet takes the least time to revolve around the sun? **Mercury**

Earth's Nearest Neighbors

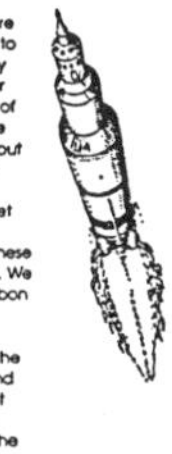

With a roar of the giant rocket engines, we are pressed tightly to our seats. We are on our way to visit Earth's closest planet neighbors. Our journey takes us first to a planet that looks much like our moon with its craters. It is Mercury, the smallest of our neighboring planets. It is only one-half of the Earth's size. There is no air on Mercury to block out the sun's extreme heat. This causes the surface temperature on Mercury to reach 400°C.

As our spacecraft continues, we sight a planet that is almost the size of Earth. This is Venus, covered with a mist of swirling, yellow clouds. These clouds are made up of droplets of sulfuric acid. We cannot land here because the air is mostly carbon dioxide and the temperature is 470°C.

Our spacecraft speeds past Earth, quickly approaching a red-colored planet about half the size of Earth. Its surface is dry and desert-like and covered with craters. This planet is Mars, with its violent dust storms. The temperature on the surface is 26°C. But we won't see any life here because the air is 100 times thinner than Earth's, and it is 95 percent carbon dioxide.

Complete the chart below using the information you gathered on your visit to the neighboring planets.

	Daytime Temperature	Size Compared to Earth	Atmosphere	Surface
Mercury	400°C	½	no air	craters
Venus	470°C	almost	CO₂	clouds
Earth	varies	same	air	oceans/mtns/desert
Mars	26°C	½	CO₂	desert craters

The Outer Planets

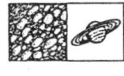

We are approaching the largest planet, Jupiter. It is eleven times wider than Earth. If it were hollow, it could hold 1,300 Earths inside! We can see Jupiter's rapidly changing bands of clouds and brilliant flashes of lightning. It is extremely warm; Jupiter gives off twice as much heat as it receives from the sun. The Great Red Spot on the surface is a tremendous storm, 14,000 km wide and 40,000 km long. It travels completely around the planet every six days. Beneath the thick clouds of Jupiter is a great, spinning ball of liquid ammonia and methane gases.

We are now approaching one of the most fantastic sights of our journey — the giant rings of Saturn. The rings consist of ice and ice-covered rock orbiting the planet. The rings are over 65,000 km wide but only a few kilometers thick. Like Jupiter, Saturn seems to be covered with a thick covering of clouds. High winds are blowing, and the temperature in the clouds is -190°C.

1. Which is the largest planet in the Solar System? **Jupiter**
2. Which is the second largest? **Saturn**
3. What are Saturn's great rings? **particles of ice and ice-covered rocks**
4. What is Jupiter's "Great Red Spot"? **a tremendous storm**
5. How are Saturn and Jupiter alike? **Both are covered with clouds.**
6. Could you live on Jupiter? Why or why not? **No. It is covered with ammonia and methane gas.**

The Edge of the Solar System

Our spaceship is approaching the greenish-blue planet of Uranus. It appears to be about four times the diameter of Earth. It has nine rings, much like Saturn's. The planet is covered with clouds that are made up of hydrogen, helium, and methane gas. As we leave Uranus, we can count five moons orbiting the planet.

We are now 4.5 billion kilometers from Earth and are approaching the eighth planet, Neptune. Neptune is similar in size to Uranus. It is also covered with a thick, cloud atmosphere of hydrogen and methane gas.

As we get nearer to Pluto, we are now at the edge of the Solar System. If we look back, our sun appears like a bright star in the sky. Pluto is so far away from the sun that the temperature is almost absolute zero, the point at which there is no heat at all!

Use the clues to fill in the puzzle and find the secret word.

1. Uranus has five _____ — **moons**
2. Planet farthest from the sun — **Pluto**
3. Planet with nine rings — **Uranus**
4. Neptune is covered with — **clouds**
5. Eighth planet from the sun — **Neptune**

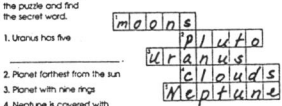

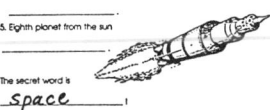

The secret word is **space**.

Comets, Asteroids, and Meteors

There are other objects in our Solar System besides planets, moons, and the sun. You might have seen some of them streaking by if you have ever stared at the evening sky.

Comets are like "dirty snowballs." A comet is made up of frozen gas (the snow) and dust particles (the dirt). It shines by reflecting the sun's light as it travels in a stretched-out orbit around the sun. As a comet gets close to the sun, it melts and forms a "tail."

Between the orbits of Jupiter and Mars are thousands of rocky objects, called asteroids, orbiting the sun. Asteroids, some as large as 1,000 km across, are believed to be pieces of a planet that broke apart.

Meteors are streaks of light made by chunks of stone or metal traveling through Earth's atmosphere and burning up. If a meteor strikes the Earth, it is called a meteorite. Some people call meteors "shooting stars."

Complete the chart by placing a (✓) in the appropriate box.

	Meteor	Asteroid	Comet
frozen ball of dust			✓
orbits the sun		✓	✓
shooting star	✓		
burns up in Earth's atmosphere	✓		
orbits between Mars and Jupiter		✓	
appears as a streak in the sky	✓		
is visible in our sky	✓		✓

© Instructional Fair, Inc.   IF0233 Science Enrichment

The Solar System

Label the different parts of the Solar System: the sun, the planets, the comet, and the asteroids.

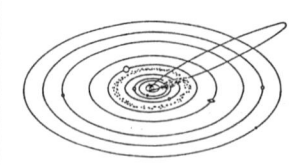

Extra
Research the planets to learn about their size and density. Order them from smallest to largest here.

1. Pluto
2. Mercury
3. Mars
4. Venus
5. Earth
6. Neptune
7. Uranus
8. Saturn
9. Jupiter

Magnitude

The stars that you see on a clear night seem to be closer than they really are. Light from the sun, the closest star to Earth, takes 8.3 minutes to reach us. Light from the next closest star, Proxima Centauri, takes 4.3 years to reach us. Proxima Centauri is not even visible without the aid of a telescope.

All of the stars in the sky do not look alike. The most visible difference is in the brightness of the stars. The measure of brightness is called magnitude. The magnitude of a star is determined by its size, distance from Earth, and its temperature.

Stars are balls of hot gases. The color of a star helps us determine its temperature. Red stars are the coldest stars, with a surface temperature of 3,000°C. The hottest stars that can be seen are blue stars. Their temperature is over 20,000°C. White stars are over 10,000°C. Our sun is a yellow star with a surface temperature of 5,500°C.

Use what you have learned about temperature and star color to color the stars.

red 3,000°C yellow 5,000°C white 10,000°C blue 20,000°C

What three factors determine a star's magnitude?
size   distance from Earth   temperature

Two stars are the same color and distance from Earth, but their size is different. Which star will have the greater magnitude?
The larger of the two.

Star Heat

Use the information from the chart to make a graph showing the temperature of the four stars.

Star	Color	Temperature
Rigel	Blue-white	12,000°C
Sun	Yellow	5,500°C
Betelgeuse	Red	3,000°C
Sirius	White	10,500°C

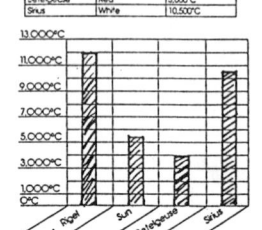

A Star Is Born

The changes in a star's life take place over billions of years. Let's look at the stages of a typical star. A star is formed from a swirling nebula, or cloud of dust and gas, in space. The forces of gravity press the matter in the nebula together. When the matter is pressed tightly enough, it gets hotter and hotter, until a new star is born. This new star is large and cool – although cool is 3,000°C. The new star has a red glow.

If the star continues to compress, the matter may become one of several different colors: blue, white, yellow, or red. In terms of star heat, this is hot, warm, lukewarm, or cool. Our sun is a yellow star. It is hotter than a red star, but cooler than a white star.

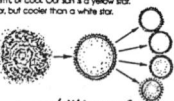

1. How long is the life span of a star? billions of years
2. What is a nebula? swirling cloud of dust & gas
3. What color is the sun? yellow
4. Which color stars are hotter than our sun? Cooler than our sun?
Blue and white are hotter. Red is cooler.

Number the stages of the birth of a star in the correct order.
4 The matter in the young star continues to compress and get hotter.
1 The nebula is a swirling mass of dust and gas.
3 The newly born star is a cool 3,000°C.
2 Gravity forces dust and gases of the nebula to press together.
5 The star becomes a new color as it gets hotter.

Star Death

As stars get older, they go through changes. A star begins "old age" when its central core of hydrogen has become all helium. Its energy source is gone. Gravity squeezes the center core tight, while the outer layers begin to expand and cool to a dull red. The star becomes a red giant.

The outer layer forms a ring nebula that disappears into space leaving behind a super-collapsed core, about the size of a planet. The core becomes hotter as it collapses and forms a small, white star called a white dwarf. The white dwarf is so dense that a teaspoon of material would weigh almost one ton.

Because the white dwarf has no energy left, it grows dimmer and dimmer until it is a cold, black sphere called a black dwarf.

As you grow older, you can see changes over periods of months and years. You can't see the changes in stars. Stars change over periods of millions, and sometimes billions, of years.

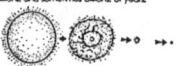

1. Why do stars die? They die because their energy is gone.
2. Could you see a black dwarf? Why or why not? No, because it no longer gives off light.

Number the stages of a dying star in the correct order.
4 The white dwarf becomes cooler and dimmer.
2 The outer layer of the star expands while the core squeezes tight, forming a red giant.
5 The star becomes a cold, black sphere in space.
1 The star uses its last remaining supply of hydrogen.
3 The outer layer of the red giant forms a ring nebula.

Black Holes

Imagine a star with gravity so strong that nothing can escape from it, not even light. These stars are called black holes.

When a massive star begins to burn out, it collapses. A star ten times the size of the sun will shrink to a sphere about 60 km in diameter. It becomes so dense and the gravitational pull so strong, that the star disappears! Anything that passes close to it in space will be sucked in and never get out!

How do astronomers look for black holes if they can't be seen? They look indirectly. A black hole pulls in matter from nearby stars. As the matter disappears, it sends out strong bursts of x-rays. Astronomers look for these x-ray signals. The most promising candidate for a black hole is the x-ray source known as Cygnus X-1.

Secret Message
The black hole below has swallowed some of the planets of the Solar System. Shade in the names of the planets. The letters that are not shaded will help you solve the secret message.

IF BLACK HOLES EXIST, NOBODY CAN SEE THEM.

Pictures in the Stars

On a clear night, lie on your back and gaze up at the hundreds of twinkling stars. Try to imagine different pictures by drawing lines from star to star. Hundreds of years ago, people drew pictures with the stars in the same way. These pictures are called constellations.

Many of the constellations get their names from Greek mythology. One well-known constellation of the winter skies is Orion, the mighty hunter of Greek mythology.

We can use constellations to help locate special stars. The Big Dipper is a constellation that can help you locate Polaris, the North Star. With your eye, make an imaginary line from the two stars on the end of the Dipper's cup. This line will point to Polaris.

1. What is a constellation? It is an imaginary picture made with stars.
2. How can a constellation be helpful to the stargazer? They can help you locate specific stars.

Many constellations are hard to picture. Below are the four star patterns that are also shown above. Identify each constellation by its common name.

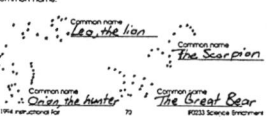

Leo, the Lion
The Scorpion
Orion, the hunter
The Great Bear

The Zodiac

Ancient astronomers noticed that certain constellations always came up in the east just before sunrise. This was because they were found in the same belt which was traced by the sun across the sky. The path made by these constellations actually formed a belt that circled around the heavens. This belt was divided into twelve equal parts, each containing one major constellation.

Most of the constellations that appeared in the belt were named after animals. The early Greeks called this belt Zodiakos Kyklos, or "circle of animals." We call it the Zodiac for short.

The Zodiac was eventually called the horoscope, known as astrologers, to tell the fortune of a person born under a particular Zodiac sign. (Each Zodiac sign is associated with a specific time period in the year.) The reading by an astrologer is called a horoscope.

Circle the Latin names of the twelve constellations of the Zodiac in the wordsearch.

Word Bank
Aquarius   Libra
Aries   Pisces
Cancer   Sagittarius
Capricorn   Scorpio
Gemini   Taurus
Leo   Virgo

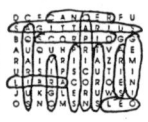

Match each Latin name with its English translation.
Aries   The Ram
Taurus   The Bull
Gemini   The Twins
Cancer   The Crab
Leo   The Lion
Virgo   The Virgin
Libra   The Scales
Scorpio   The Scorpion
Sagittarius   The Archer
Capricorn   The Goat
Aquarius   The Water Carrier
Pisces   The Fish

Space Puzzle

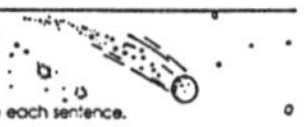

Use the Word Bank to complete each sentence.

Word Bank
astronomer   fusion   Mercury   orbit   sun
Earth   hydrogen   meteorite   Pluto   Centauri
fall   maria   moon   shuttle   axis

1. A star's energy comes from nuclear fusion
2. The only planet with life is Earth
3. The path of a planet around the sun is its orbit
4. Earth's largest satellite is moon
5. The autumnal equinox is the first day of fall
6. The planet farthest away from the sun is Pluto
7. The closest planet to the sun is Mercury
8. A meteor that lands on the earth is a meteorite
9. A scientist who studies the Universe is an astronomer
10. A star's fuel is hydrogen
11. The star closest to the earth is the sun
12. Oceans on the moon are called maria
13. A space shuttle is a reusable space craft.
14. The closest star to our solar system is Proxima Centauri
15. The imaginary line from the North Pole to the South Pole is the Earth's axis

Joe's Tooth: The Inside Story

Use your science book or another source to help.

Word Bank

neck	crown	enamel	dentin
root	cementum	pulp	

Label the inside parts of Joe's tooth using the Word Bank.

Label the outside parts of Joe's tooth using the Word Bank.

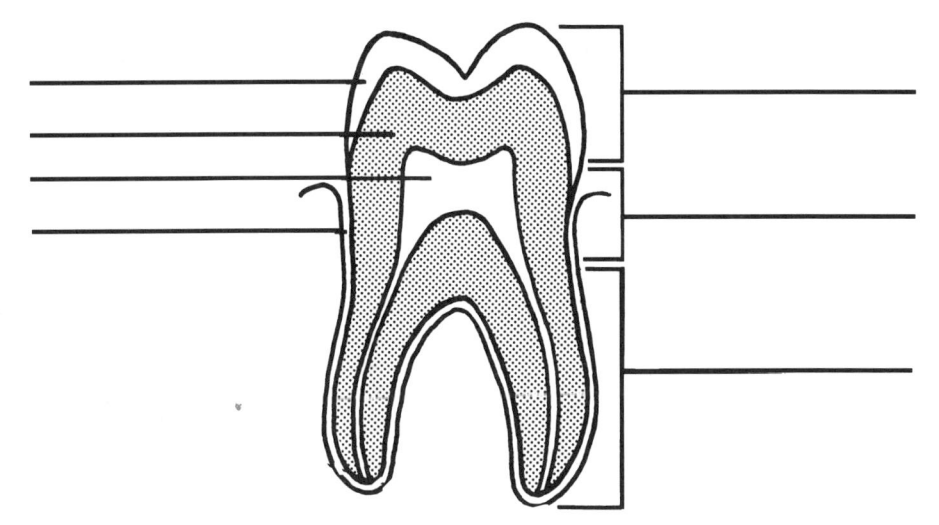

Tooth Puzzle
Complete the puzzle using the Word Bank.

Across
2. The outer covering of the tooth's roots
4. The hard, bone-like layer of the tooth
7. The part of the tooth located above the gum

Down
1. Soft tissues, blood vessels, and nerves that fill the inside space of the tooth
3. The tough, outer layer of the tooth
5. The part of the tooth between the crown and the root
6. The part of the tooth embedded in the jaw

© 1994 Instructional Fair

IF0233 Science Enrichment

Nibblers and Chompers

Use your science book or another source to help.
Fill in the spaces with words from the Word Bank.

You have four kinds of _____ in your mouth, each with a special job. The large, front teeth are called _____ . The incisors are the nippers that help you bite into an apple. The sharp pointy teeth are _____ . Canines are used to tear food, like when you chew meat off a bone. The _____ are large teeth with two points. The _____ are the large, flat teeth in the back of your mouth. Both the bicuspids and molars are the ``millstones'' used for grinding food.

Label the teeth on the diagram by printing the following letters on the teeth:

I = Incisors   C = Canines   B = Bicuspids   M = Molars

Word Bank

canines
bicuspids
incisors
molars
teeth

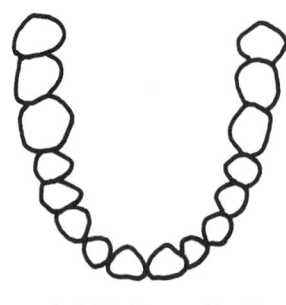

Adult's Upper Teeth   Adult's Lower Teeth

© 1994 Instructional Fair   IF0233 Science Enrichment

Cough! Cough!

What makes your heart beat faster, replaces the oxygen in your blood with carbon monoxide, makes your blood pressure shoot up, and leaves deadly chemicals in your body – and all in just three seconds? If you answered, ''cigarettes,'' then you are right.

When you inhale smoke, it travels down your windpipe and into your bronchial tubes. These tubes are covered with hair-like parts called **cilia**. The cilia move back and forth, trying to sweep the smoke dust back up the throat. Cough! Cough! The dust and dirt are out of your body. But cigarette smoke stops these hairs from doing their work. As a result, your lungs become lined with tar. This tar contains chemicals that are harmful to your body.

Cough! Cough! Is your body trying to tell you something?

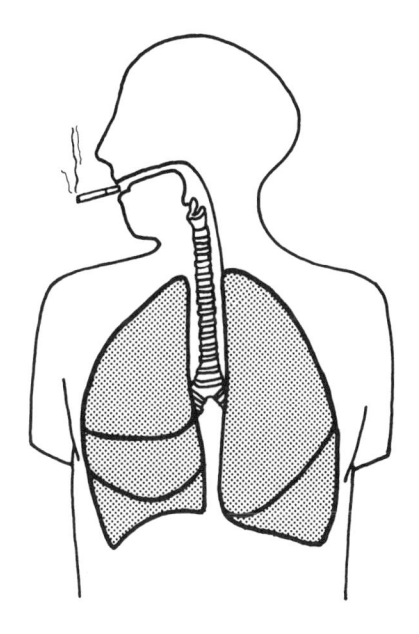

What are three excuses people use for smoking?

1. _____
2. _____
3. _____

What are three reasons why people should not smoke?

1. _____
2. _____
3. _____

Body Trivia

Test your knowledge of the human body with these amazing facts.

Across
1. 105 sweat glands are found in one square centimeter of your _____.
3. Your heart pumps 6,000 liters of this each day.
5. Hardest substance in the human body
6. The average person has 100,000 of these on his/her head.
8. You do this with your eyes.
10. Your mouth makes 1/2 liter of this each day.
12. Smallest bones of the body are located here.
13. You breathe 12,000 liters of this each day.
14. Filters 1,500 liters of blood each day
15. It takes more of these to frown than to smile.

Down
2. 17 times more light comes through an expanded one than a narrow one.
3. At birth you have 300, but in adulthood you have 206.
4. "Stomach" rumbles occur here.
6. Strongest muscle in your body
7. Only part of the body with taste buds
9. They give you stereo vision.
11. Receives 100 million nerve messages from your senses each second

© 1994 Instructional Fair

Solid to the Core?

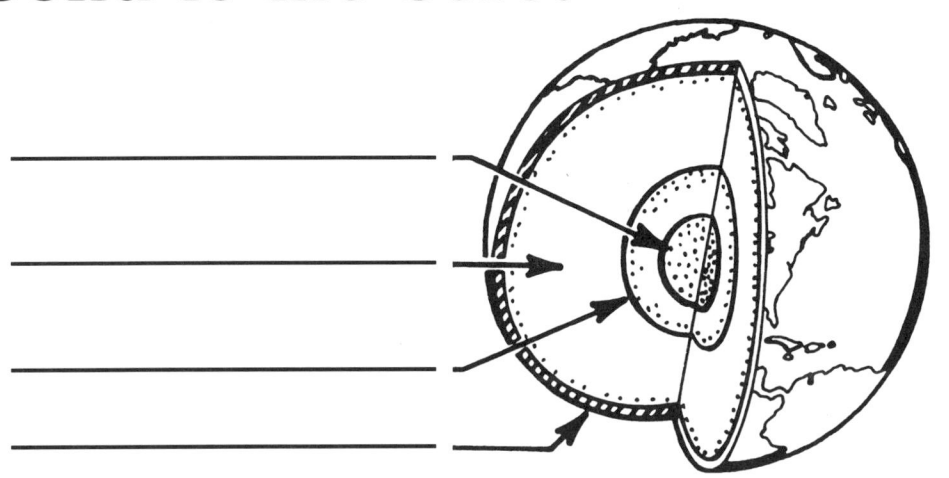

_____

_____

_____

_____

Like a peach, the Earth has three layers. You can compare the outer layer, or **crust**, of the Earth to the peach's skin. It is a thin crust of hard rock, from 5 to 70 kilometers thick.

Beneath the crust is the **mantle**. Like the fleshy part of the peach, it is the thickest layer. The mantle is made of very hot rock that is not liquid, but plastic-like and soft. The mantle is almost 3,000 kilometers thick.

The innermost layer of the earth, the **core**, is like the peach's pit. The **outer core** is liquid and most likely made of iron. The outer core is about 2,000 kilometers thick. The **inner core** is solid and seems to be made of iron and nickel. The inner core is 1,500 kilometers thick.

• Use the words in bold above to label the layers of the Earth.

1. How far is it from the surface to the center of the Earth? _____
   _____

2. The Earth's crust is _____ kilometers thick.

3. The inner core is made from iron and _____ .

4. The outer core is made of _____ .

5. The innermost layer of the Earth is called the _____ .

© 1994 Instructional Fair   41   IF0233 Science Enrichment

Land Beneath the Ocean

The land beneath the ocean has features that are very similar to those that you would see if you traveled across North America.

- Study the picture of the ocean floor. First label the picture and then the descriptions below, using the words from the Word Bank.

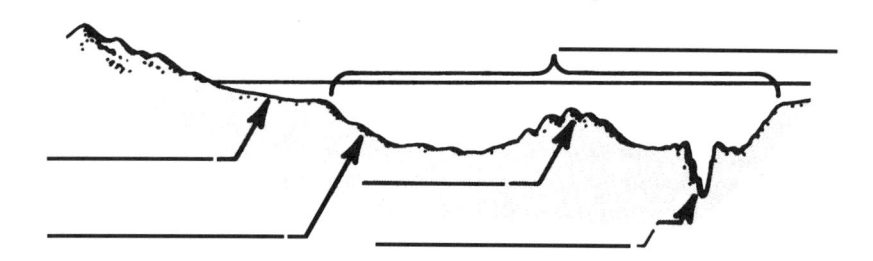

Word Bank

mid-ocean ridge	ocean basin
continental slope	trench
continental shelf	

1. _____ A narrow, deep valley in the ocean basin.

2. _____ A steep incline at the edge of the continental shelf.

3. _____ A chain of mountains on the ocean floor.

4. _____ The part of the ocean floor nearest the continents.

5. _____ The deepest part of the ocean which contains valleys, plains, and mountains.

"Ping-Ping"

The depth of the ocean can be measured using a device called an echo sounder. A sound, "ping," is sent from a ship to the ocean floor. The length of time it takes for the "ping" to strike the ocean floor and bounce back to the ship is recorded. Sound travels in water at a speed of 1,500 meters per second. If a ping takes 6 seconds for a round trip, then a one way trip must take 3 seconds. The depth of the ocean at that point must be 4,500 m (3 sec. x 1,500 m/sec. = 4,500 m).

1. Find the various depths of the ocean using the "ping" soundings on this chart.

2. Using the depths you have listed on the chart, graph your results on the chart below. Connect the points to make a profile of the ocean floor.

3. Put a * on the deep ocean trench.

4. Put an X on the continental slope.

5. Put an M on the undersea mountain.

Sounding	Time (sec.)		Speed (m/sec.)		Depth (m)
1	.4	X	1,500	=	600
2	.4	X	1,500	=	600
3	3	X	1,500	=	
4	2.6	X	1,500	=	3,900
5	3	X	1,500	=	
6	2	X	1,500	=	
7	1	X	1,500	=	
8	2	X	1,500	=	
9	3	X	1,500	=	
10	3.4	X	1,500	=	5,100
11	2	X	1,500	=	
12	7	X	1,500	=	
13	1	X	1,500	=	

Depth

Sea Level
1,000 m
2,000 m
3,000 m
4,000 m
5,000 m
6,000 m
7,000 m
8,000 m
9,000 m
10,000 m
11,000 m

Sounding 1 2 3 4 5 6 7 8 9 10 11 12 13

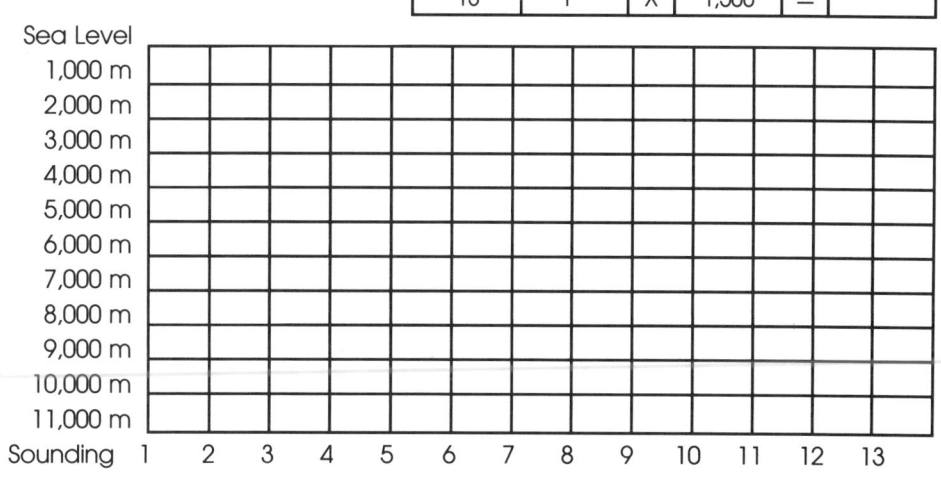

© 1994 Instructional Fair

Fire Rocks

Deep inside the Earth the intense heat causes some rocks to melt. This molten rock, called **magma**, rises toward the surface of the Earth because it is less dense than solid rock. Magma that flows onto the Earth's surface is called **lava**. Some magma cools before it reaches the Earth's surface, forming **igneous** rocks.

Many different types of igneous rocks can be formed, depending on how fast the magma or lava cools. When melted rock cools quickly, very small crystals are formed, causing the new rock to appear glassy. When molten rock cools slowly, large crystals are formed.

Solve the puzzle, matching each rock with its description in the Word Bank. Use what you have read above and information from other sources.

1. Melted rock that comes out of the Earth.
2. Melted rock that cooled quickly, forming a black, glassy rock.
3. Greenish-black rock, formed from lava that flowed slowly over the surface.
4. Formed from lava that cooled with hot gases trapped inside, causing it to be filled with air holes.
5. Melted rock below the Earth's surface.
6. Magma that cooled slowly, forming large crystals.
7. Lava that cooled slowly, forming large crystals.

Word Bank

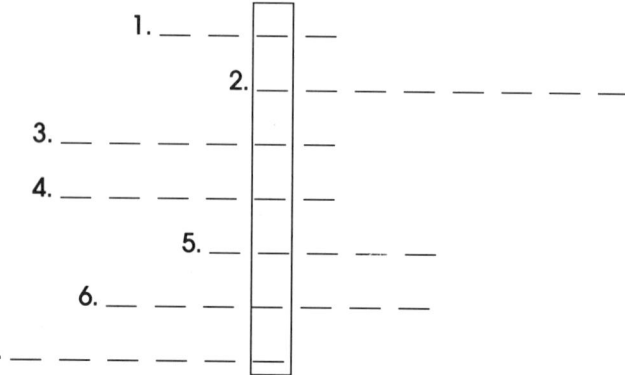

pumice	gabbro
granite	magma
lava	obsidian
basalt	

The hidden word: What is a mountain formed by cooled lava?

Stones of Sand

As rivers flow to the sea, they may carry mud, sand, pebbles, and boulders along the way. The river drops this material, called **sediment**, into the sea. As layers of sediment build up over a period of many years, the great pressure of all these layers changes the sediment into **sedimentary rock**.

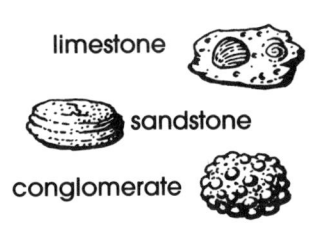

limestone

sandstone

conglomerate

Many different types of sedimentary rock can be formed, depending on the material that is found in the sediment.

- Use what you have read above and your science book to help you match the sedimentary rocks with their description.

_____ 1. Layers and layers of sand are deposited on the sea bottom to form this rock.

_____ 2. A mixture of sand and small pebbles is "cemented" together to form this rock.

_____ 3. Living plants in a swamp are covered with sediment and pressed, eventually forming this valuable source of energy.

_____ 4. Small sea animals and shells are pressed into this kind of rock.

_____ 5. Layers of mud form the most common type of sedimentary rock.

a. sandstone

b. shale

c. limestone

d. conglomerate

e. coal

- Sediments settle at different rates of speed. Number these elements in the order that they would settle.

_____ pebbles   _____ boulders   _____ sand

Changing Rocks

With enough pressure and heat, sedimentary and igneous rock can be changed into a new rock. This new kind of rock is called **metamorphic**, which means "changed in form."

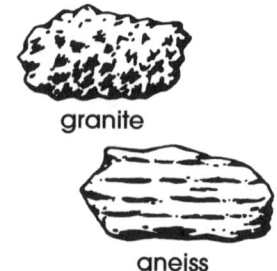

There are a number of ways that metamorphic rock can be formed. One way is when rocks that are buried deep under the Earth's surface are flattened by the great pressure from above them. An example of this is when granite is changed into gneiss. Look carefully at the pictures. How has the appearance of the granite changed?

granite

gneiss

Rock Cycle

Look closely at the rock cycle diagram. This cycle shows how rock material is mixed and re-used again and again.

Unscramble the terms to show examples of how igneous and sedimentary rocks can change into metamorphic rock.

1. _ _ _ _ _ changes into _ _ _ _ _ .
   H E S A L   T A L E S

2. _ _ _ _ _ _ _ changes into _ _ _ _ _ _ .
   T R I N E G A   S I N E G S

3. _ _ _ _ _ _ _ _ _ changes into _ _ _ _ _ _ .
   M O E S T E L N I

   into _ _ _ _ _ _ .
   B E L M A R

Testing Minerals

All minerals have certain characteristics, or properties, which distinguish them from other minerals. Minerals can be identified by the testing of these properties. A scratch test is used to determine the property of **hardness**. Minerals are rated on a scale of one to ten - one is the softest and ten the hardest.

It usually takes many more than one property to identify a mineral, but let's try our skill using the hardness test.

Hardness Number	Test	Mineral
1	Fingernail scratches it easily	talc
2	Fingernail barely scratches it	gypsum/kaolinite
3	Copper penny scratches it	calcite/mica
4	Glass scratches it easily	fluorite
5	Steel knife will scratch it easily	apatite/hornblend
6	It will scratch glass	feldspar
7	It will scratch a steel knife	quartz
8	It will scratch a steel file	topaz
9	It will scratch topaz	corundum
10	It will scratch corundum	diamond

1. It will scratch glass (glassy, colorless). _____

2. Copper penny scratches it (pearly, colorless). _____

3. Copper penny scratches it (pearly, black). _____

4. Fingernail barely scratches it (glassy, gray). _____

5. It will scratch glass (glassy, gray). _____

6. Fingernail barely scratches it (dull, yellow). _____

7. Steel knife will scratch it (glassy, black). _____

8. Fingernail scratches it easily (pearly, white). _____

© 1994 Instructional Fair IF0233 Science Enrichment

It's California's Fault!

There are many cracks in the Earth's bedrock. These cracks are called **faults**. One kind of fault is called a **strike-slip fault**. The rock along one side of the fault moves horizontally in one direction, while the facing rock moves in the opposite direction. Other times, the bedrock on one side of the fault moves upward, while the other side moves down. This is called a **dip-slip fault**.

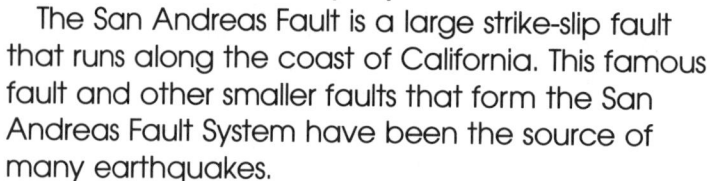

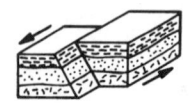

The San Andreas Fault is a large strike-slip fault that runs along the coast of California. This famous fault and other smaller faults that form the San Andreas Fault System have been the source of many earthquakes.

1. Label the two types of faults using the words in bold above.
2. On which side of the San Andreas Fault is San Francisco?

3. On which side of the San Andreas Fault is Santa Cruz?

4. The San Andreas Fault's movement has been measured to be as much as 5 cm per year. What might happen to these two cities a million years from now?

Ring of Fire

Deep inside the Earth, melted rock called **magma** moves toward the Earth's surface. When the magma reaches the surface, it is called **lava**.

In a volcano, the magma travels through a tube-like passageway called a **conduit**, until it reaches an opening in the Earth's surface, called a **vent**. This vent may be in the top of the mountain or it could be a **side vent**. Sometimes the lava flows out gently, but other times it may explode.

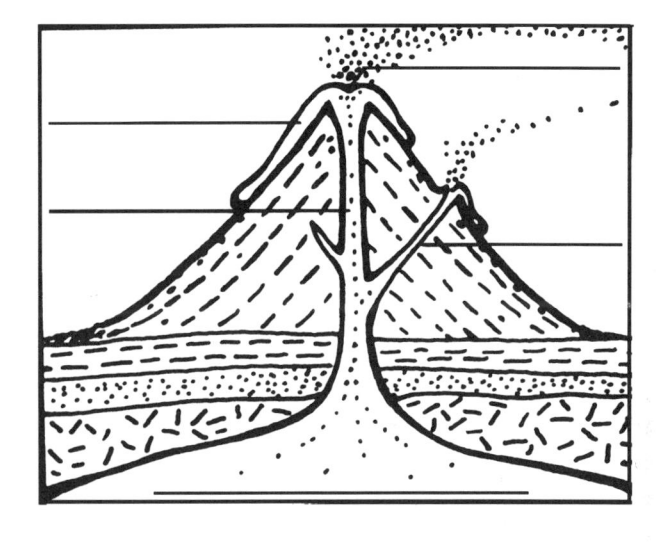

Volcanoes can occur wherever there is a deep crack in the Earth's surface. Most volcanoes occur in a large belt that encircles the Pacific Ocean. This belt is called the **Ring of Fire**.

- Label the parts of the volcano using the words found in bold above.
- Fill in the blanks to show the types of material that come out of a volcano.

1. Rocks with sharp corners that are blown out from the inside of a volcano: __ __ __ __ __ __ .

2. Lava blown into the air, cools into small coarse pieces of rock which are puffed up by gas: __ __ __ __ __ __ .

3. Magma that has reached the surface: __ __ __ __ .

Word Bank

| blocks | cinder | lava |

Shake, Rattle, and Roll!

An earthquake is a movement in the Earth's crust. The large blocks of rock along a fault (a crack in the earth) slip past each other. As the blocks of rock slide, their sides may become locked. The strain builds and then becomes too great, causing the rocks to quickly slip past each other. The result is an earthquake. From the origin of the earthquake, called the **focus**, waves, or vibrations, move out in all directions.

Earthquakes are recorded on a sensitive instrument called a **seismograph**. The strength of the earthquake is measured on a scale of 1 to 10, with 10 being the strongest. This scale is called the **Richter Scale**.

Mexico City	2,600 km
Denver	1,400 km
Vancouver	1,600 km

- Seismographs in three cities were able to record the same earthquake. The data showed that the focus of the earthquake was located at different distances from each of the cities. For each city, set your compass for the distance indicated. Draw a circle using the city as its center. Mark the focus by placing an **X** on the map where the three circles meet.

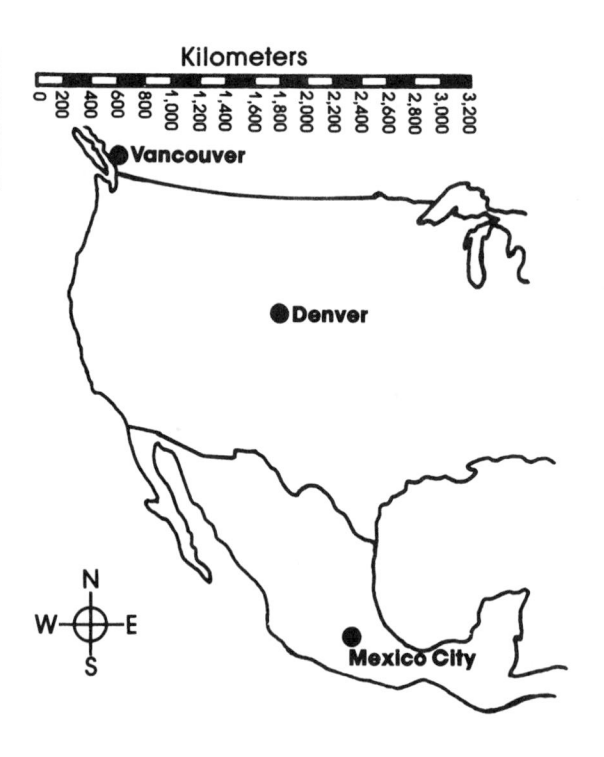

1. Where do earthquakes usually occur?

_____

2. Why might some earthquakes be stronger than others?

Mountain Building

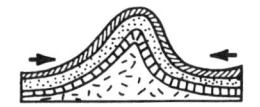

_____ _____ _____

    Mammoth mountains can be found in many places throughout the world. How are these mountains formed?

    Most mountains are formed when continental plates collide with each other. The force of the plates pushing against each other causes the crust to bulge up higher and higher, until ''waves'' of mountains are formed. The mountains that are formed this way are called **folded mountains**.

    Other mountains are formed along faults. Along one side of the fault, the block of crust moves up. Along the other side of the fault, the block of crust moves down. The mountains that are formed from this are called **fault-block mountains**.

    A third type of mountain, formed much in the same way folded mountains are, is a **dome mountain**. A bulge is formed. However, the bulge is caused by magma from the earth's mantle pushing against the crust.

1. Label the drawings of mountain types using the words in bold.

2. What is the main difference between a folded mountain and a fault-block mountain?

   _____

   _____

3. What are two forces that form mountains?

   _____

   _____

Natural Fountains

Geysers, those spectacular natural fountains of spurting hot water, are actually a special kind of hot spring.

Water from rain and snow seeps thousands of meters underground. There the water is heated to 204° or higher, a temperature far above the boiling point of water. This superheated water expands and rises to the surface, where the steam bubbles escape. But from time to time, the bubbles become too abundant to pass up through the water. When this happens, so much steam builds up that the water actually explodes out of a vent in the ground, rising anywhere from 1 m to 60 m into the air.

Yellowstone National Park is known for its geysers and hot springs. Listed below are a few of those geysers.

Geyser	Height	Duration	Interval
Artemisia	9 m	13-15 min.	24-30 hrs.
Beehive	45 m	5-8 min.	2-5 days
Great Fountain	60 m	35-60 min.	5-17 hrs.
Grotto	12 m	1-2 hrs.	1-12 hrs.
Lion	18 m	4 min.	1-2 hrs.
Old Faithful	56 m	2-5 min.	33-95 min.
Riverside	23 m	20 min.	6-9 hrs.
Steady	5 m	steady	steady

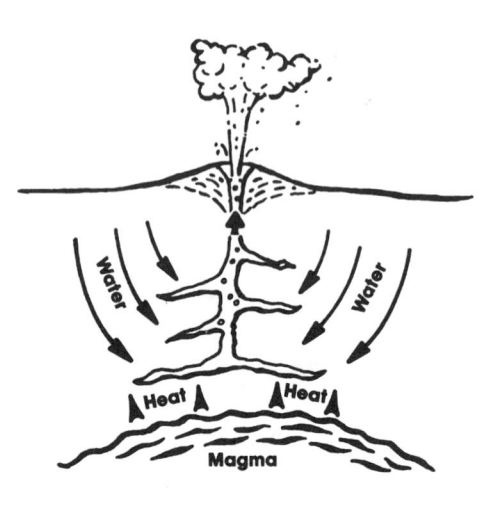

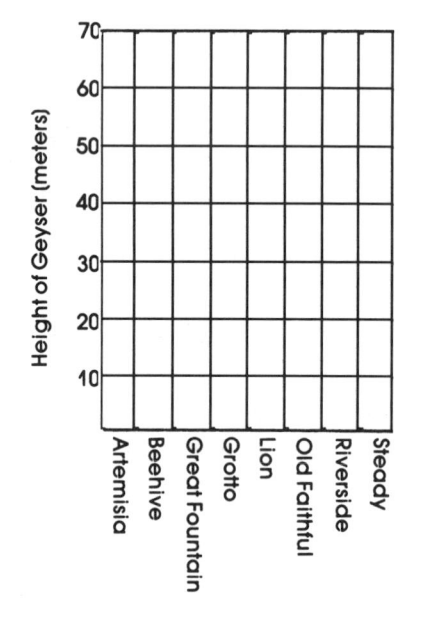

1. Graph the height of each geyser.

2. Which geyser erupts the most often? _____

© 1994 Instructional Fair   IF0233 Science Enrichment

Rivers of Ice

Ice
Bedrock   Snow   Moraine

A large mass of snow and ice that lasts for years and years is called a **glacier**. Glaciers form over a period of years when more snow falls in the winter than melts in the summer. As the snow accumulates, the snow deep under the surface snow compresses into thick, dense ice. This ice, called **firn**, can be from 30 to 50 meters thick.

In mountainous regions, the downward pull of gravity on the ice causes the flow down the mountainside. As the solid glacier flows, it picks up rocks and stones. When the glacier melts, the rocks and stones are deposited in small mounds called **moraines**.

- The force of a glacier has left these glacial terms in a bit of a mess. Unscramble them. You may consult your science book or another resource book.

Glacier formed long smooth hills. __ __ __ __ __ __ __ __
                                                        D M L R U N I S

Refrozen snowmelt in a glacier. __ __ __ __
                                         F N I R

Large crack in a glacier. __ __ __ __ __ __ __ __
                            S R A C E S E V

Melted glacial ice. __ __ __ __ __ __ __ __ __
                       M T W T E A L E R

Small mound formed by the deposit of rocks from a melting glacier. __ __ __ __ __ __ __
                                                                R O M I N A E

Just Plain Dirt

Soil is made of pieces of rocks and minerals that have been broken down by nature over a period of thousands of years.

Soil is found in three layers. The top layer, where plants usually grow, is called **topsoil**. The second layer, which contains pebbles, sand, and clay, is called **subsoil**. The bottom layer contains large rocks and is called **bedrock**.

• How is soil formed? _____
_____

• The foundation of a very large building often goes all the way down to the bedrock. Why?
_____
_____

Soil	Structure	Properties
Sand	Small pieces of quartz	Does not hold water
Clay	Very small pieces of mineral other than quartz	Holds water very well
Loam	Sand, clay, and humus (decayed plants and animals)	Holds water yet drains

Tell what type of soil you would choose in each situation below. The chart will help you.

1. Garden _____ Why? _____
_____

2. Bottom of a man-made pond _____ Why? _____

© 1994 Instructional Fair IF0233 Science Enrichment

Earth Shattering Review

Down
1. Small mound formed by a deposit of rocks from a glacier.
3. Movement in the Earth's crust caused by the slipping of large blocks of rock along a fault.
6. Rocks formed by layers of sediment under great pressure.
8. Remains or imprints of organisms left in sedimentary rock.
9. A narrow, deep valley in the ocean basin.

Across
2. Rocks that are changed in form.
4. The thin outer layer of the Earth.
5. Rocks formed by the cooling of magma.
7. The innermost layer of the Earth.
8. A crack in the Earth's surface.
10. Molten rock beneath the surface of the Earth.
11. Layer of rock between the Earth's core and crust.

Word Bank

magma	earthquake	metamorphic
lava	focus	igneous
moraine	sedimentary	coal
mantle	fossils	trench
crust	fault	core

© 1994 Instructional Fair

Our Moon

On July 20, 1969, Neil Armstrong and Edwin Aldrin left the first footprints on the moon. The astronauts found our moon to be without air, water, plants, or any living things.

The moon is covered with billions of bowl-shaped holes called **craters**. Scientists believe the craters were formed when objects traveling in space hit and dented the moon's surface.

When you look at the moon with a telescope, you will see large, flat, smoother areas. Early astronomers believed that these areas were oceans. They called the areas **maria**, which means ''seas'' in Latin. Actually, there is no water on the moon. Maria are dry lava beds that were formed by volcanic action on the moon about 3½ million years ago.

Pretend you are an astronaut preparing for a visit to the moon. Decide which items from the list below would be needed or not needed for your visit. Give your reasons.

Item	Needed	Not Needed	Reason
signal whistle			
matches			
water			
raincoat			
lightweight equipment			
oxygen			
food			

Changing Faces

Have you ever noticed that the moon's face appears to have different shapes at different times of the month? These changes in shape are called the moon's **phases**. Of course, the moon does not actually change shape, nor does it produce its own light. Do you know what accounts for the moon's shape and light?

As the moon revolves around the Earth, we can see different amounts of the moon's lighted part. Study the drawing of the moon's different phases carefully.

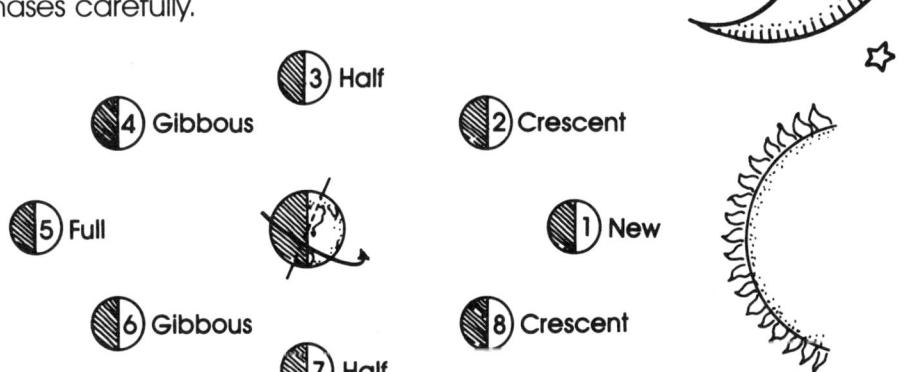

3) Half
4) Gibbous
2) Crescent
5) Full
1) New
6) Gibbous
8) Crescent
7) Half

Draw each of the moon's phases as seen from Earth. Label each phase.

1	2	3	4
5	6	7	8

© 1994 Instructional Fair   IF0233 Science Enrichment

Space Shadows

Objects in space often cast shadows. Sometimes the moon passes between the Earth and the sun. The moon slowly blocks out the sun's light, casting a shadow on the Earth. The sky gets dark, the air cools, and for several minutes you can see the stars. This is a **solar eclipse**.

As the moon travels around the Earth, sometimes the Earth will cast a shadow on the moon. The full moon darkens as it moves into the Earth's shadow. This eclipse, which will last for over an hour, is called a **lunar eclipse**.

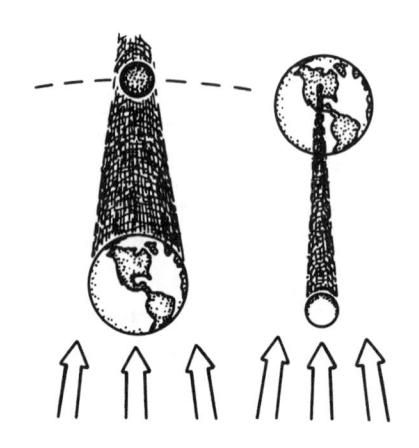

Draw the position of the moon and the shadows for both the solar and lunar eclipses. Label each picture.

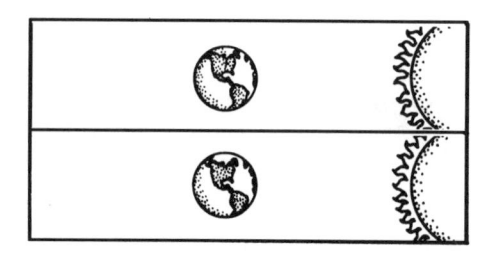

Complete the following chart by checking the correct box for each statement.

	Lunar Eclipse	Solar Eclipse
Earth casts a shadow		
moon casts a shadow		
takes place at night		
takes place during the day		
moon is blocked out		
sun is blocked out		
causes the sky to get dark		
causes the air to cool		

© 1994 Instructional Fair   IF0233 Science Enrichment

Exploring Our Solar System

You can learn much about the planets in our Solar System by studying the table on this page. Use the information from the table to answer the questions.

Planet	Diameter	Distance from the Sun	Revolution	Rotation
Mercury	4,880 km	57,900,000 km	88 days	59 days
Venus	12,100 km	108,200,000 km	225 days	243 days
Earth	12,756 km	149,600,000 km	365 days	24 hours
Mars	6,794 km	228,000,000 km	687 days	24.5 hours
Jupiter	143,200 km	778,400,000 km	11.9 years	10 hours
Saturn	120,000 km	1,425,600,000 km	29.5 years	11 hours
Uranus	51,800 km	2,867,000,000 km	84 years	16 hours
Neptune	49,500 km	4,486,000,000 km	164 years	18.5 hours
Pluto	2,600 km	5,890,000,000 km	247 years	6.5 days

1. Which planet is closest to the sun? _____

2. Which planet is farthest from the sun? _____

3. Which planets are located between Earth and the sun? _____
_____

4. Which is the largest planet? _____

5. Which is the smallest planet? _____

6. What is the diameter of Earth? _____

7. How long does it take for Pluto to revolve around the sun? _____

8. Which planet takes the least time to revolve around the sun? _____

Earth's Nearest Neighbors

With a roar of the giant rocket engines, we are pressed tightly to our seats. We are on our way to visit Earth's closest planet neighbors. Our journey takes us first to a planet that looks much like our moon with its craters. It is **Mercury**, the smallest of our neighboring planets. It is only one-half of the Earth's size. There is no air on Mercury to block out the sun's extreme heat. This causes the surface temperature on Mercury to reach 400°C.

As our spacecraft continues, we sight a planet that is almost the size of Earth. This is **Venus**, covered with a mist of swirling, yellow clouds. These clouds are made up of droplets of sulfuric acid. We cannot land here because the air is mostly carbon dioxide and the temperature is 470°C.

Our spacecraft speeds past Earth, quickly approaching a red-colored planet about half the size of Earth. Its surface is dry and desert-like and covered with craters. This is **Mars**, with its violent dust storms. The temperature on the surface is 26°C. But we won't see any life here because the air is 100 times thinner than Earth's, and it is 95 percent carbon dioxide.

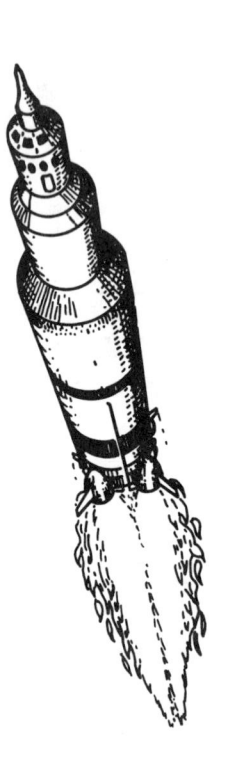

Complete the chart below using the information you gathered on your visit to the neighboring planets.

	Daytime Temperature	Size Compared to Earth	Atmosphere	Surface
Mercury				
Venus				
Earth				
Mars				

© 1994 Instructional Fair IF0233 Science Enrichment

The Outer Planets

We are approaching the largest planet, **Jupiter**. It is eleven times wider than Earth. If it were hollow, it could hold 1,300 Earths inside! We can see Jupiter's rapidly changing bands of clouds and brilliant flashes of lightning. It is extremely warm; Jupiter gives off twice as much heat as it receives from the sun. The Great Red Spot on the surface is a tremendous storm, 14,000 km wide and 40,000 km long. It travels completely around the planet every six days. Beneath the thick clouds, Jupiter is a great, spinning ball of liquid ammonia and methane gases.

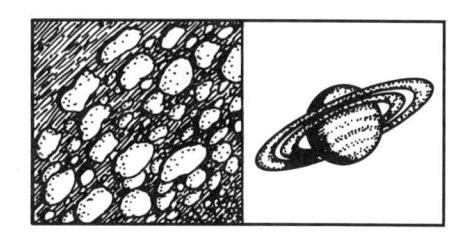

We are now approaching one of the most fantastic sights of our journey - the giant rings of **Saturn**. The rings sparkle in the sunlight as they circle the glowing, yellow planet. As we get closer to the rings, we notice that they are actually particles of ice and ice-covered rock orbiting the planet. The rings are over 65,000 km wide but only a few kilometers thick. Like Jupiter, Saturn seems to be covered with a thick covering of clouds. High winds are blowing, and the temperature in the clouds is -190°C.

1. Which is the largest planet in the Solar System? _____

2. Which is the second largest? _____

3. What are Saturn's great rings? _____

4. What is Jupiter's ``Great Red Spot''? _____

5. How are Saturn and Jupiter alike? _____
_____

6. Could you live on Jupiter? Why or why not? _____
_____

The Edge of the Solar System

Our spaceship is approaching the greenish-blue planet of **Uranus**. It appears to be about four times the diameter of Earth. It has nine rings, much like Saturn's. The planet is covered with clouds that are made up of hydrogen, helium, and methane gas. As we leave Uranus, we can count five moons orbiting the planet.

We are now 4.5 billion kilometers from Earth and are approaching the eighth planet, **Neptune**. Neptune is similar in size to Uranus. It is also covered with a thick, cloud atmosphere of hydrogen and methane gas.

As we get nearer to **Pluto**, we are now at the edge of the Solar System. If we look back, our sun appears like a bright star in the sky. Pluto is so far away from the sun that the temperature is almost absolute zero, the point at which there is no heat at all!

Use the clues to fill in the puzzle and find the secret word.

1. Uranus has five _____.

2. Planet farthest from the sun

3. Planet with nine rings

4. Neptune is covered with _____.

5. Eighth planet from the sun

_____

The secret word is

_____!

Comets, Asteroids, and Meteors

There are other objects in our Solar System besides planets, moons, and the sun. You might have seen some of them streaking by if you have ever stared at the evening sky.

Comets are like "dirty snowballs." A comet is made up of frozen gas (the snow) and dust particles (the dirt). It shines by reflecting the sun's light as it travels in a stretched-out orbit around the sun. As a comet gets closer to the sun, it melts and forms a "tail."

Between the orbits of Jupiter and Mars are thousands of rocky objects, called **asteroids**, orbiting the sun. Asteroids, some as large as 1,000 km long, are believed to be pieces of a planet that broke apart.

Meteors are streaks of light made by chunks of stone or metal traveling through Earth's atmosphere and burning up. If a meteor strikes the Earth, it is called a meteorite. Some people call meteors "shooting stars."

Complete the chart by placing a (✓) in the appropriate box.

	Meteor	Asteroid	Comet
frozen ball of dust			
orbits the sun			
shooting star			
burns up in Earth's atmosphere			
orbits between Mars and Jupiter			
appears as a streak in the sky			
is visible in our sky			

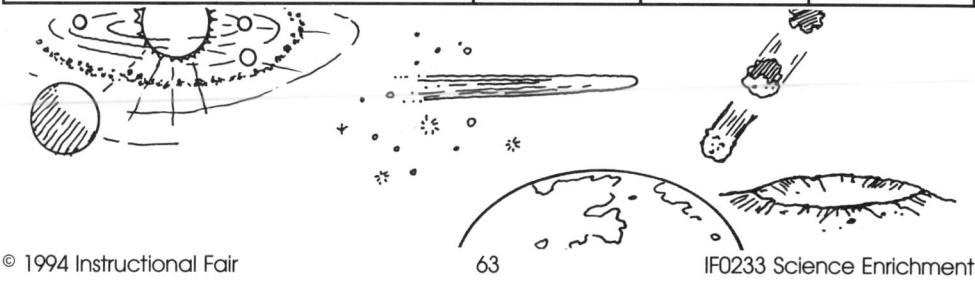

The Solar System

Label the different parts of the Solar System: the sun, the planets, the comet, and the asteroids.

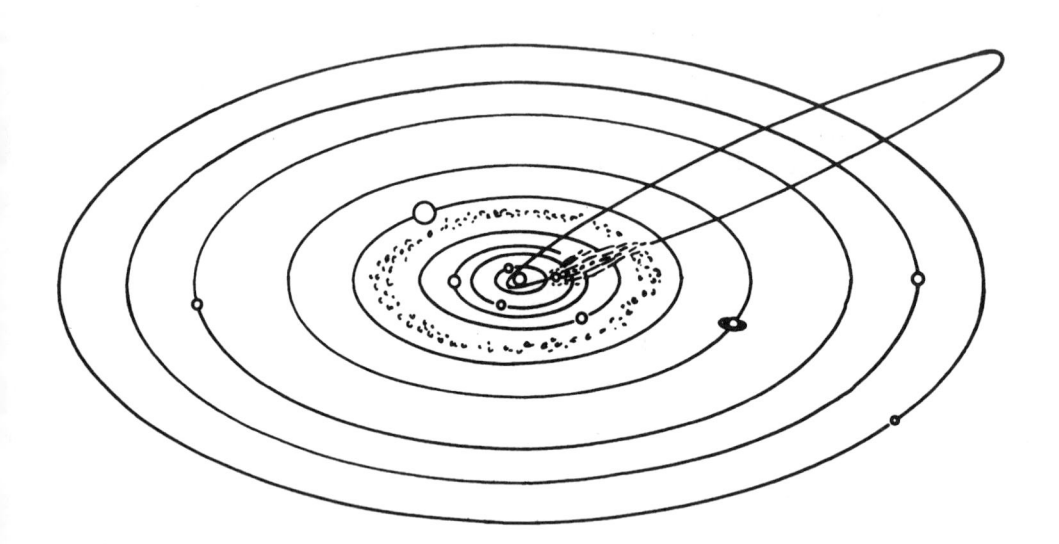

Extra
Research the planets to learn about their size and density. Order them from smallest to largest here.

1. _____
2. _____
3. _____
4. _____
5. _____
6. _____
7. _____
8. _____
9. _____

© 1994 Instructional Fair　　　　　IF0233 Science Enrichment

Magnitude

The stars that you see on a clear night seem to be closer than they really are. Light from the sun, the closest star to Earth, takes 8.3 minutes to reach us. Light from the next closest star, Proxima Centauri, takes 4.3 years to reach us. Proxima Centauri is not even visible without the aid of a telescope.

All of the stars in the sky do not look alike. The most visible difference is in the brightness of the stars. The measure of brightness is called **magnitude**. The magnitude of a star is determined by its size, distance from Earth, and its temperature.

Stars are balls of hot gases. The color of a star helps us determine its temperature. Red stars are the coldest stars, with a surface temperature of 3,000°C. The hottest stars that can be seen are blue stars. Their temperature is over 20,000°C. White stars are over 10,000°C. Our sun is a yellow star with a surface temperature of 5,500°C.

Use what you have learned about temperature and star color to color the stars.

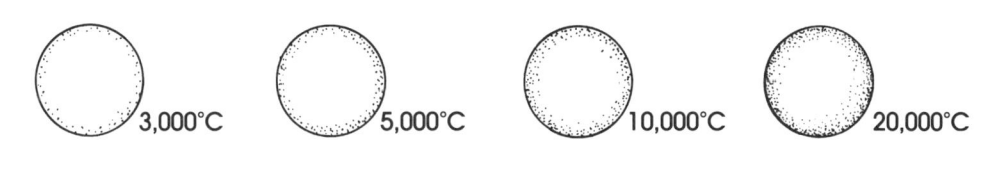

◯ 3,000°C   ◯ 5,000°C   ◯ 10,000°C   ◯ 20,000°C

What three factors determine a star's magnitude?

_____   _____   _____

Two stars are the same color and distance from Earth, but their size is different. Which star will have the greater magnitude?

_____

_____

Star Heat

Use the information from the chart to make a graph showing the temperature of the four stars.

Star	Color	Temperature
Rigel	Blue-white	12,000°C
Sun	Yellow	5,500°C
Betelgeuse	Red	3,000°C
Sirius	White	10,500°C

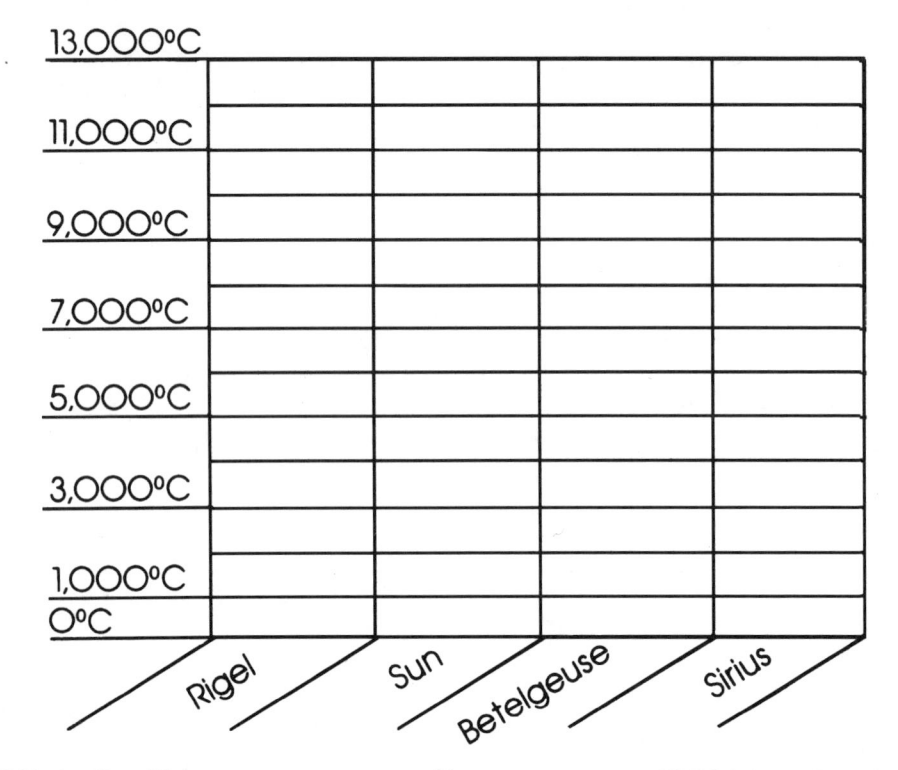

A Star Is Born

The changes in a star's life take place over billions of years. Let's look at the stages of a typical star. A star is formed from a swirling **nebula**, or cloud of dust and gas, in space. The forces of gravity press the matter in the nebula together. When the matter is pressed tightly enough, it gets hotter and hotter, until a new star is born. This new star is large and cool - although cool is 3,000°C. The new star has a red glow.

If the star continues to compress, the matter may become one of several different colors: blue, white, yellow, or red. In terms of star heat, this is hot, warm, lukewarm, or cool. Our sun is a yellow star. It is hotter than a red star, but cooler than a white star.

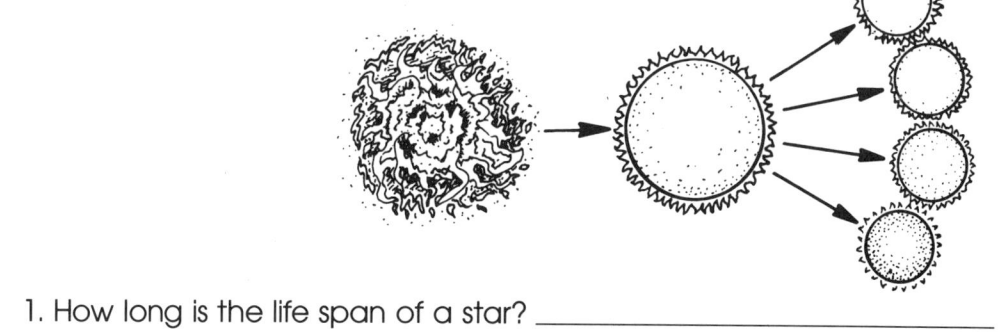

1. How long is the life span of a star? _____

2. What Is a nebula? _____

3. What color is the sun? _____

4. Which color stars are hotter than our sun? Cooler than our sun?
   _____
   _____

Number the stages of the birth of a star in the correct order.

_____ The matter in the young star continues to compress and get hotter.

_____ The nebula is a swirling mass of dust and gas.

_____ The newly born star is a cool 3,000°C.

_____ Gravity forces dust and gases of the nebula to press together.

_____ The star becomes a new color as it gets hotter.

© 1994 Instructional Fair IF0233 Science Enrichment

Star Death

As stars get older, they go through changes. A star begins "old age" when its central core of hydrogen has become all helium. Its energy source is gone. Gravity squeezes the center core tight, while the outer layers begin to expand and cool to a dull red. The star becomes a **red giant**.

The outer layer forms a ring nebula that disappears into space leaving behind a super-collapsed core, about the size of a planet. The core becomes hotter as it collapses and forms a small, white star called a **white dwarf**. The white dwarf is so dense that a teaspoon of material would weigh almost one ton.

Because the white dwarf has no energy left, it grows dimmer and dimmer until it is a cold, black sphere called a **black dwarf**.

As you grow older, you can see changes over periods of months and years. You can't see the changes in stars. Stars change over periods of millions, and sometimes billions, of years.

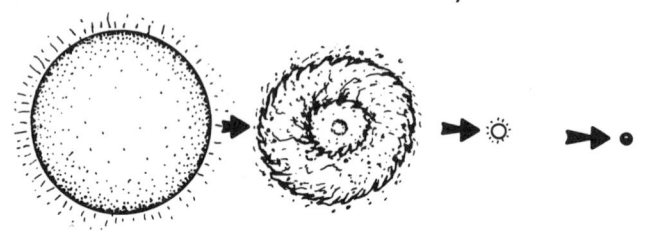

1. Why do stars die? _____

_____

2. Could you see a black dwarf? Why or why not? _____

_____

Number the stages of a dying star in the correct order.

_____ The white dwarf becomes cooler and dimmer.

_____ The outer layer of the star expands while the core squeezes tight, forming a red giant.

_____ The star becomes a cold, black sphere in space.

_____ The star uses its last remaining supply of hydrogen.

_____ The outer layer of the red giant forms a ring nebula.

Black Holes

Imagine a star with gravity so strong that nothing can escape from it, not even light. These stars are called **black holes**.

When a massive star begins to burn out, it collapses. A star ten times the size of our sun will shrink to a sphere about 60 km in diameter. It becomes so dense and the gravitational pull so strong, that the star disappears! Anything that passes close to it in space will be sucked in and never get out!

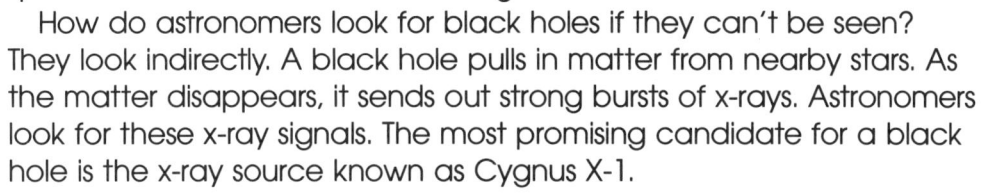

How do astronomers look for black holes if they can't be seen? They look indirectly. A black hole pulls in matter from nearby stars. As the matter disappears, it sends out strong bursts of x-rays. Astronomers look for these x-ray signals. The most promising candidate for a black hole is the x-ray source known as Cygnus X-1.

Secret Message

The black hole below has swallowed some of the planets of the Solar System. Shade in the names of the planets. The letters that are not shaded will help you solve the secret message.

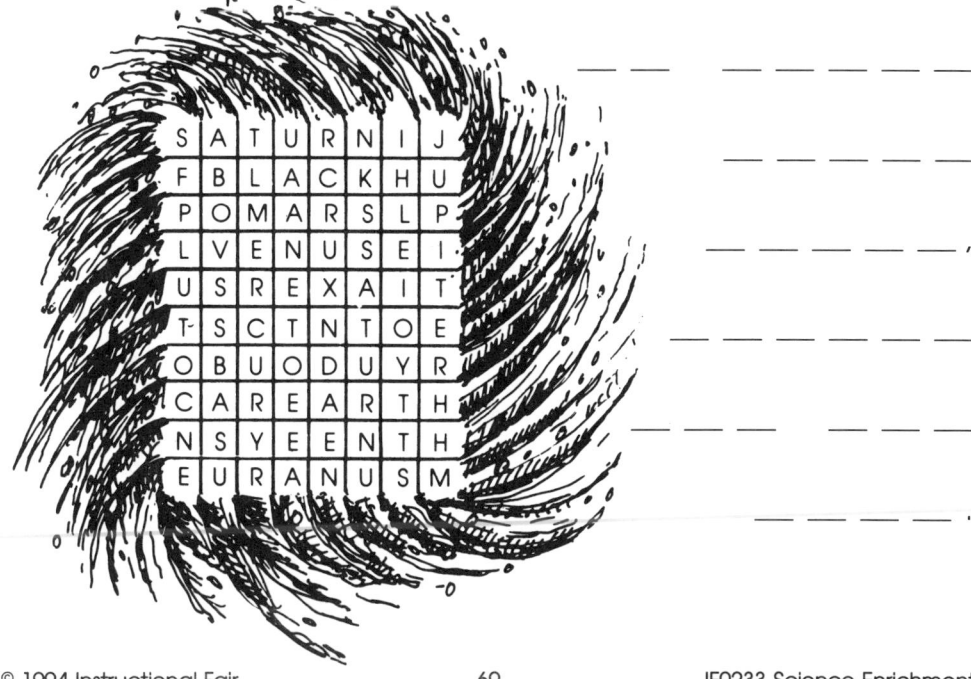

S	A	T	U	R	N	I	J
F	B	L	A	C	K	H	U
P	O	M	A	R	S	L	P
L	V	E	N	U	S	E	I
U	S	R	E	X	A	I	T
T	S	C	T	N	T	O	E
O	B	U	O	D	U	Y	R
C	A	R	E	A	R	T	H
N	S	Y	E	E	N	T	H
E	U	R	A	N	U	S	M

_ _ _

_ _ _ _

_ _ _ _ _ _ ,

_ _ _ _

_ _ _ _ _

_ _ _ _ .

Pictures in the Stars

On a clear night, lie on your back and gaze up at the hundreds of twinkling stars. Try to imagine different pictures by drawing lines from star to star. Hundreds of years ago, people drew pictures with the stars in this same way. These pictures are called **constellations**.

Many of the constellations get their names from Greek mythology. One well-known constellation of the winter skies is Orion, the mighty hunter of Greek mythology.

We can use constellations to help locate special stars. The Big Dipper is a constellation that can help you locate Polaris, the North Star. With your eye, make an imaginary line from the two stars on the end of the Dipper's cup. This line will point to Polaris.

1. What is a constellation? _____
   _____

2. How can a constellation be helpful to the stargazer? _____
   _____

Many constellations are hard to picture. Below are the four star patterns that are also shown above. Identify each constellation by its common name.

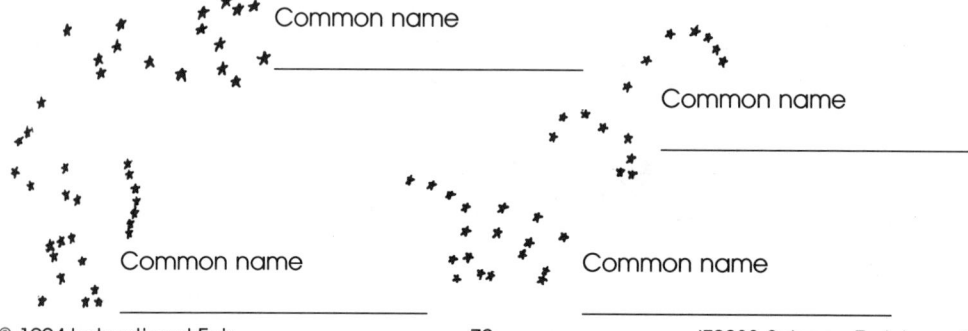

Common name _____

Common name _____

Common name _____

Common name _____

The Zodiac

Ancient astronomers noticed that certain constellations always came up in the east just before sunrise. This was because they were found in the same path that was traced by the sun across the sky. The path made by these constellations actually formed a belt that circled around the heavens. This belt was divided into twelve equal parts, each containing one major constellation.

Most of the constellations that appeared in this belt were named after animals. The early Greeks called this belt **Zodiakos Kyklos**, or "circle of animals." We call it the **Zodiac** for short.

The Zodiac was eventually used by fortune-tellers, known as astrologers, to tell the fortune of a person born under a particular Zodiac sign. (Each Zodiac sign is associated with a specific time period in the year.) The reading by an astrologer is called a **horoscope**.

Circle the Latin names of the twelve constellations of the Zodiac in the wordsearch.

Word Bank

Aquarius	Libra
Aries	Pisces
Cancer	Sagittarius
Capricorn	Scorpio
Gemini	Taurus
Leo	Virgo

```
D C E C A N C E R F U
S A G I T T A R I U S
B Q S C O R P I O G G
A U Q U H P R T V A E
R A I V R I I A Z R M
U R S I P S C U T I I
L I B R A C O R O E N
J U K G L E R U W S I
O S N O M S N S L E O
```

Match each Latin name with its English translation.

_____ The Ram   _____ The Scales

_____ The Bull   _____ The Scorpion

_____ The Twins   _____ The Archer

_____ The Crab   _____ The Goat

_____ The Lion   _____ The Water Carrier

_____ The Virgin   _____ The Fish

© 1994 Instructional Fair

Space Puzzle

Use the Word Bank to complete each sentence.

Word Bank

astronomer	fusion	Mercury	orbit	sun
Earth	hydrogen	meteorite	Pluto	Centauri
fall	maria	moon	shuttle	axis

1. A star's energy comes from nuclear _____.
2. The only planet with life is _____.
3. The path of a planet around the sun is its _____.
4. Earth's largest satellite is _____.
5. The autumnal equinox is the first day of _____.
6. The planet farthest away from the sun is _____.
7. The closest planet to the sun is _____.
8. A meteor that lands on the earth is a _____.
9. A scientist who studies the Universe is an _____.
10. A star's fuel is _____.
11. The star closest to the earth is the _____.
12. Oceans on the moon are called _____.
13. A space _____ is a reusable space craft.
14. The closest star to our solar system is Proxima _____.
15. ~~An im~~aginary line from the North Pole to the South Pole is the _____.